Every Cheese Has a Story

CASEUS

FROMAGERIE BISTRO COOKBOOK

Every Cheese Has a Story

jason sobocinski

LYONS PRESS
Guilford, Connecticut
An imprint of Globe Pequot Press

Lyons Press is an imprint of Globe Pequot Press.

Project editor: David Legere
Text design: Nancy Freeborn

Photos by Mike Toth with the exception of: p. xii (photo by Jason Sobocinski); p. 2, 15, 13, 16–17, 23, 25, 33, 43, 55, 61, 69, 93, 95, 107 (photos by Sarah Lasley).
Illustrations and cover photo by Cromack Odea.

Library of Congress Cataloging-in-Publication Data is available on file.

ISBN 978-0-7627-6118-0

Printed in the United States of America

10 9 8 7 6 5 4 3 2 1

CONTENTS

PREFACE

Hello. Caseus. How can I help you?

I'd like to make a reservation for tonight.

Excellent. What time?

Seven o'clock.

Sorry, we can't do seven. How about eight-thirty?

OK, that sounds good. What's the dress code over there? Can I wear jeans?

Only if you cut them up real high to show off your assets!

[Silence, then chuckles] *Alright then! Thanks! See you tonight!*

That's what we're about at Caseus—good times, great food, a touch of sass, and a relaxed, fun atmosphere that makes you feel like you're in your Uncle's basement over summer vacation, sneaking a stash of fireworks or a *Playboy.* Doesn't make sense? Come by for a beer and some poutine—you'll get it.

In my family my Nana always cooked. So did Mom—in fact, Dad cooked too, but mostly only his famous pancakes on Sunday mornings (still does). I was always interested in food, relegating me to the classification of "husky" size during my prepubescent years. Every Friday night Nana came over and cooked with us. I say *with us* because we were always all in the kitchen. Everyone had a job to do, and we spent real time together talking, pinching tastes, and making

suggestions on how to improve dishes that'd been made the same way for as long as anyone could remember. Usually it was pasta with anchovies (pasta *al-eeesh-zz*) or cod stewed in tomatoes or my favorite, pasta *fahzoool*—always exceptionally simple and simply wonderful no matter what. This always happened on a Friday night, and I looked forward to it all week. Dessert would be Fortissmo red wine with fresh or canned peaches. It's an abominable jug wine, the grape variety known only as "red," and where it's made will always be a mystery . . . and every sip tastes like my Poppy.

My education at Boston University (master's degree in gastronomy) was wonderful on a theoretical level, an academic exploration of cultures and their foodways—an anthropological look into how food defines different people, the uses of food outside of the context of nutrition, and to some degree a little bit of the "blah blah blah" that comes with any higher education. My education at Formaggio Kitchen in Cambridge, Massachusetts, was so much more. I learned to bake confections, cakes, and breads with Alice, the baker who'd been, and still is, with Formaggio for over fifteen years. I learned to use organic, local, and all-natural ingredients, how to procure and purvey from the most stubborn suppliers, and the art of selling not just cheese, but all of the exceptionally fine goods the store had to offer.

Formaggio had professors in all subjects: Tom Smith, the butcher and charcuterie; Michael Fitzhenry, the BBQ pit master; Eduardo, the head chef whose Puerto Rican heritage poked through with his exceptional wet chicken rub (I'd steal the pope's nose off every chicken the man roasted and savor the pop of hot schmultz and crisp skin); Christine Yates, whose aesthetic touch made everything she cooked a piece of art without looking fancy or pretentious; and Greg, the produce guy, who is still my very good friend and Ham Bomb compatriot! Phillip Conroy taught me the importance of terroir in wine over grape variety, and Ihsan Gurdal taught me how to run a successful business: His knowledge and

stubbornness never made sense until I had to deal firsthand with the sometimes huge pile of shit that success can leave at your feet.

My cheese education was headed up by Bob the Dutchman and Robert Aguliera. Robert's passion for cheese and the way he described it was enchanting. I'd listen to him talk and watch customers drink it in—we'd all be intoxicated by the way they'd buy cheese from him. Robert also taught me affinage, the art of keeping and aging cheeses and how to store them so they develop the correct balance of moisture and complexity, all in an effort to better serve the customer and provide the best product possible. His passion and dedication to the cheese industry is unmatched in my eyes, and he is still and always will be a mentor to me.

ORIGINALLY FROM NEW HAVEN, I began coming back from Boston on weekends to look at properties to hold my business, all the while working with my little brother Tommy on the Caseus website. I knew what I wanted it to be, but had no idea what it would become. Initially, all I wanted was to open a small cheese shop that would retail cheeses, premade sandwiches, and some other takeaway items. The plan was to have an extensive cheese and charcuterie selection and to use those goods to make salads, sandwiches, and soups.

My realtor, Noah Meyer, and I had exhausted just about all of the properties in the downtown New Haven area. Then he told me he wanted to show me another space—it was a disaster, in the nicest sense. We'd chosen to come while the present tenant was closed on a Sunday afternoon. When Noah flicked on the light in the kitchen, it was accompanied by the shrill scream of a large rat that had been stuck to a paper trap. It must have fallen asleep or given up, but the light had jolted it back into action. We both ran out of the place waving our hands about our heads as if to brush off any spiders, rats, or snakes that'd somehow made their way onto us. We locked the door and didn't go back for another week. Two weeks later I signed the lease on what is now Caseus Fromagerie Bistro in that very location.

WHY CHEESE? The difference between an industrial cheese made for nothing but filler and the real thing is so obvious that there is no possibility of deception. Why cheese? Because it's the perfect food, one of the building blocks of civilization, and, simply, damn delicious. Besides, what else can you melt and eat? The discovery of fermented foods—beer, bread, wine, and cheese—opened a new realm of possibilities for human civilization. These foods are possibly the most important scientific discoveries ever made by humankind to date. By realizing the potential of fermented foods and their ability to preserve, people gained power over their food. With the ability to maintain food storage, the first forms of civilization were able to blossom.

Right now we are going through another great change within our foodways with the advent of genetically modified and industrialized foods. Cheese is not immune to this change. But this change also spawned a food revolution: the creation of a great counterculture of artisans devoted to making food using the best possible methods to yield not only the best-tasting food, but also positively impact our environment and our physical health.

If asked how I want people to feel about Caseus, who we are and what we do, I'd want them to say we make people feel comfortable—not just in their stomachs and minds, but an overall feeling. When it comes to Caseus, we don't want any pretensions; the food, on the other hand, can border on pretentious, but only if you're not really paying attention to its preparation and delivery. Caseus the restaurant and this book are extensions of our family's kitchen table. Within these pages you'll not only share our recipes, but our philosophy. You'll also meet our staff, our favorite suppliers, and even some of our customers. We're not the most polished group, but we all love food and view eating as not just getting full, but rather one of life's true pleasures.

In many ways, Caseus came about so that I could enjoy with a clear conscience the foods I so love, knowing they've been made with the most natural ingredients, sourced locally with minimal impact on the environment. This way I can eat things like *poutine*—french fries laced with fresh cheese curds, *velouté* (a gravy made of chicken stock and cream), and roux. It's not a healthy dish, but when made with organic free-range heritage chicken stock, real potatoes peeled and cut fresh and fried in pure peanut oil, and locally fresh-made cheese curds, it's just not as bad for you!

So come on in. You'll hear a cornucopia of rock, reggae, blues, jazz, punk, and later on, when there are only a few tables left, old-school hardcore rap thumping through our little speakers, placed right next to our phone and reservation board. The music ebbs and flows when the phone rings; it's a good time, I assure you.

Jason

Cheeseboards, 4

Charcuterie Boards, 7

Chicken Liver & Foie Gras Mousse, 11

Poutine, 12

Duck Sliders w. Epoisse & Dried Figs, 14

Deep-Fried Sweetbreads w. Artichokes,
Radicchio & Lemon Feta, 16

Leek & Goat Cheese Tart, 18

Lamb Sliders w. Neal's Yard Dairy Colston
Bassett Stilton & Pea Shoots, 22

Bread & Butter, 24

SMALL PLATES

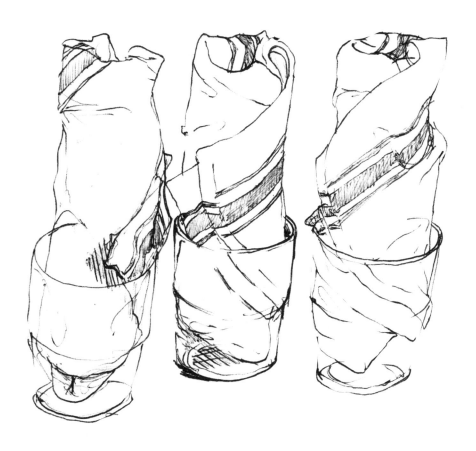

Smaller Plates

...oards

an ide...
...Having
...ult as
...dible

1-Tart Du Jo...
1-venison pot pie

...have a...
...anim...
...es of c...
...our bo...
...ct of a...
...as a con...
...d and th...
...th bread
...a cheese...

Date:
Time: 9...

Sara...
TABLE

THE LITTLE THINGS WE LOVE TO SCARF DOWN are some of our all-time favorites. Sometimes just a simple cheeseboard, a charcuterie board, or a little tart can be just as satisfying as a big, elaborate meal. Our small plates are small in more than just size. They are limited in number of ingredients, time of preparation, and explanation in most cases. The key is getting the best possible quality in ingredients, knowing where they are from and why they are so wonderful. What these dishes lack in size they make up for in big, full flavors that satiate the heartiest appetites while their explanations satisfy the most finicky gastronomes.

Serve an array of these dishes together as a tapas-style meal or at a cocktail party. Using singled out, bold flavors with less elaborate techniques makes for more precious and precise eating (with more praise from your guests) and leaves you with less cleanup after dinner. This style of eating has always been a favorite of mine because I get to try more types of food at one seating. Plus, who can deny that when going out or even eating at home, it's the little bits, appetizers, and nibbles that are most satisfying?

cheeseboards

LESS SO A RECIPE AND MORE SO AN IDEA, a cheeseboard is by far the most versatile and simple dish that can come out of your kitchen. Having said that, throwing several cheeses together with no thought or passion will yield the same result as a plastic supermarket platter of fanned-out orange, white, and yellow squares on a bed of inedible curly parsley.

Our cheeseboards attempt to have a different theme each night. Each has enough cheese to satiate two diners as a pre- or post-meal accompaniment, or the perfect amount for a nice lunch alongside a cold beer.

Combining four different types of cheese—goat, cow, sheep, and a blue—is the best plan of attack. More than four cheeses on your board can cause confusion among the varied flavors. And while flavors are the most important aspect of a cheeseboard, varying textures are essential to a successful board as well.

Think of a cheeseboard as a composition. All of the variables should be balanced and thought out in a clearly defined context. A cheeseboard is not simply a hunk of cheese with bread and mustard. That's a snack—a plowman's lunch—and can be damn near the perfect meal, but a cheeseboard has more to it. Rather, a cheeseboard is a crescendo of flavors that complement each other while still staying true to themselves. A cheeseboard primes the palate for what is to come or completes what just was.

Before-dinner cheeseboards and after-dinner cheeseboards are horses of a different color. When people come into the Caseus cheese shop looking for cheese for a dinner party, the first question I ask is, "Is this for before or after dinner?" My next question is, "What are you having?" The type of cheese you serve depends entirely on the timing and the meal. For example, if you're having roast leg of lamb, I'd recommend a brebis. For grilled salmon, a fresh chèvre. For roast beef, a robust washed rind, such as Munster Haxaire. For pork chops, Cabot Clothbound Cheddar accompanied by an apple Mostarda.

OUR BOARDS

When Caseus was being built, Tom Cocco headed up the skilled portion of most of the construction. Tom, my wife Kelly's uncle, is a boisterous, fun-loving carpenter who loves exotic woods. He'd just finished up a deck job using Brazilian mahogany (also known as IPE) and had several lengths of scrap in his garage. When I saw them one day, I asked him if I could use them for the cheese and charcuterie boards. They've been a staple in Caseus ever since, and we even have reproductions of them for sale in our cheese shop. While IPE is *not* a sustainable wood, unfortunately, our boards are leftover scraps from large decking jobs; making use of them helps to combat waste of this amazing wood, known for its brilliant color and soft texture.

Bonnie's Jams
Raspberry
Rich and delicious with
cream and sandwiches
Ingredients: ripe raspberries,
sugar and lemon juice
Net wt. 8.75oz 248g
3 8 5 7 5
Refrigerate after opening
bonniesjams.com

The weather also factors into the decision. Is it raining and cold? If so, go with a hearty Scharfer Maxx from Switzerland. Hot and sticky? Go for some sheep's milk feta with a drizzle of olive oil and a squeeze of lemon juice.

A great way to start a dinner party is with a single small forma goat cheese such as Valençay, Pouligny, or Charolais. Just put the whole piece out on a small board with a knife, and greet your guests with something bubbly. Slightly aged goat cheeses are light yet are interesting in both flavor and aesthetics, making them a great conversation starter. The best tip I can give you: Everyone likes wine with bubbles.

After dinner is the perfect time for a pungent blue, just before a fudgy chocolate cake, or a hunk of briny Parmigiano Reggiano, drizzled with honey and dusted with freshly ground black pepper, to prepare your palate for a warm bread pudding or custard.

At Caseus, a goat's milk cheese, typically the lightest in texture and flavor, starts most of our boards. A sheep's or cow's milk would be next in line, depending on the style. A stinky washed-rind cow's milk would move to the third slot to make room for a nutty, buttery brebis. Last in line, at fourth spot, would be a pungent, spicy blue.

Remember that cheeseboards are intended not to satisfy huge appetites, but more to awaken the palate and enlighten the senses with their array of flavors from real farmstead and artisanal cheeses. Use the highest quality cheeses you can find to have guaranteed success in the compilation of your boards.

charcuterie boards

Food writer Michael Ruhlman calls charcuterie the craft of salting, smoking, and curing. I call it delicious and one of my favorite categories of food. Charcuterie first came about as a way to preserve meats before refrigeration hit the scene. Now its main function is to take cuts of meat that are typically less desirable and turn them into star attractions able to stand up as flavor powerhouses on any menu.

Cured meats, like cheeses, are a home run when it comes to easy entertaining—simply enjoying food as it's made to be without doing anything but presenting it. Curing your own prosciutto is a possibility, but it is better left in the hands of the artisans. It's like this: I can't fabricate a Porsche, but I'd certainly like to drive one. What I'm saying is that I am in no way telling you not to go out and make your own pâté or cure your own salumi. Can you? Absolutely you can. But can you do it as well as the great artisans that make it available to you? No offense, but it's doubtful. I like to mix my charcuterie board with a few items I've made as well as a few made by a great charcutier.

As with the cheeseboards, the K.I.S.S. (keep it simple stupid) method is the way of the walk. Don't have more than four different selections on a board. Too many cured meats are never a bad thing, but it can get overwhelming and muddle flavors. Make boards small and simple with the highest possible quality you can find, and add your own touches as often as possible.

Good charcuterie boards have a balance of meats accompanied by pickled vegetables, always some form of mustard, and crusty bread for

Bacon technically falls under the umbrella of charcuterie, and bacon...well, what can I say about bacon? It's one of my all-time passions.

smearing pâtés or holding ribbons of thinly sliced *jamón*. Provide a good variety of flavors and textures: one cured meat, such as a jamón serrano, prosciutto, or coppa; one type of salume or dry cured sausage of some ilk; one course pâté with large, chewy chunks of meat; and one spreadable mousse-style pâté. This gives you the best of the salty savory meat world all on one plate or, in our case, board.

SOME NOTABLE CHARCUTIERS IN THE UNITED STATES

LA QUERCIA: Produces amazing pig products like coppa, prosciutto Americano, and pancetta using naturally raised heritage breed pigs. This is the crème de la crème of American artisan charcutiers.

MOLINARI: Produces great salami, sopressata, and small dry-cured sausages with natural mold rinds.

COLUMBUS: Produces an artisan line that uses all Niman Ranch pork products with natural mold rinds.

FRAMANI: Produces Paul Bertoli's artisan line of dry-cured sausages. Top dollar yields top products, and this line embodies that. It's well worth the extra expense.

sylvo &tom

TITLE: Mom and Dad

BIRTHPLACE: Mom: New Haven, Connecticut. Dad: Milford, Connecticut.

HOBBIES: Working in the cheese shop, listening to the Rolling Stones, gardening, photography, travel, and learning about cheese.

FAVORITE DISH TO MAKE AT HOME: Mom: My favorite dish is nonny rice. My grandmother used to make it for me—it consists of rice, eggs, milk, and butter. It's pure comfort food. Dad: Moules Frites.

WHAT DO YOU LOVE ABOUT CASEUS? It's made me a much more adventurous eater.

FAVORITE CASEUS MEAL? My favorite meal is the scallops with heirloom tomatoes in the summer and onion soup in the winter. *Yeah, yeah, yeah, I know it has beef stock.*

Cheese

Shop

↙ Downstairs

chicken liver & foie gras mousse

This dish could not be easier to make; it should take you as long to prepare as it does to sit and eat. It does require a night in the fridge, so make it a day or two ahead of when you plan to eat it. If you can't find foie gras, that's OK, but the addition of the force-fed duck livers truly elevates this mousse to the next level.

FEEDS: APPROXIMATELY 15 AS A STARTER, OR 1 PERSON OVER A WEEK'S TIME

1. Clean the livers of any sinew. Rinse and dry them thoroughly with paper towels or a kitchen towel.

2. Heat the oil in a large sauté pan over medium heat, and then add the livers and cook until they are nicely caramelized on both sides. Keep them to a medium-rare to rare.

3. While still hot, transfer livers to a food processor or blender. Add a large pinch of kosher salt and several grinds of black pepper and blend baby blend! Now blend it some more. It should be really, nicely blended!

4. In the same pan, sauté the onions, shallots, thyme, and garlic until the onions are translucent and soft. Remove the sprig of thyme.

5. Crank up the burner to high heat and add the vinegar and bourbon to the pan, scraping the pan to deglaze it. Cook until most of the liquid has dissipated. Add the still-warm mixture to the liver in the food processor.

6. Add the cream slowly to the mixture, pulsing until the mixture is nicely smooth. Add the unsalted butter a bit at a time until completely blended. Taste the mixture and adjust the seasoning. It should taste very salty while hot so that when it's cold it will taste just right. This is very important to keep it from tasting like old leather.

7. Poor the mixture into small bowls, terrines, pots, or jars. Let rest in the fridge, covered, overnight or until nicely chilled and set up. Serve with crusty bread on a charcuterie board or as a decadent spread for sandwiches.

1 pound total chicken livers and foie gras (or just chicken livers if you're feeling poor). If you do use foie gras, you only need a few ounces.

2 tablespoons olive oil

Kosher salt and freshly ground black pepper

1 medium onion, sliced

2 large shallots, thinly sliced

1 sprig fresh thyme

4 cloves garlic, peeled, smashed, and minced finely with the side of a knife

1 teaspoon Pedro Ximenez sherry vinegar

2 tablespoons bourbon

½ cup cream

¼ pound unsalted butter, room temperature and cut into chunks

A COMPLEMENT TO THE DISH

Grainy mustard and Maldon salt are key components in the dish, as well as crusty bread to make this a smash hit on any charcuterie board.

poutine

An after-hours staple in Montreal, this hearty dish is said to have been invented by Canadian truckers looking to take with them all the components of a perfect meal in a cup: cheese, gravy, and french fries. Genius. As far as I know, Caseus was the first restaurant in Connecticut to serve poutine as a menu staple. As long as we're open we'll have it, and as long as we have it I claim ours to be the best around!

FEEDS: 4–6

8 large Idaho potatoes

2 quarts or more peanut oil (for frying)

Kosher salt and freshly ground black pepper

FOR THE *POMMES FRITES* (FRENCH FRIES):

1. Peel the potatoes and cut to desired french fry shape. A quarter inch or so is nice, as they stay hearty and crisp at this size. Rinse in cold water and drain thoroughly.

2. Bring peanut oil to 300–325°F.

3. Blanch the potatoes in the hot oil for 4–5 minutes or until soft but not brown. Work in small batches so as not to cool the oil down too much. Remove potatoes and let cool to room temperature. This step is best done ahead, as far ahead as a few hours or even a day before eating. They can be stored in an airtight container in the fridge.

4. Heat oil temperature to 375–400°F.

5. In small batches, fry the blanched potatoes in the hot oil until lightly browned and crispy. Drain the hot fries on newspaper or brown paper bags. Season with salt and pepper immediately.

You only have 10 seconds to season the fries. If you wait, the salt will not properly adhere to the fries and will fall off of them. Unsalted fries are a sacrilege.

3 tablespoons fresh unsalted butter

3 tablespoons all-purpose flour

2 cups chicken stock (page 139)

1 cup fresh cream

Kosher salt and freshly ground black pepper

FOR THE VELOUTÉ:

1. In a saucepan over medium heat, melt the unsalted butter. Stir in the flour and cook for several minutes until the roux is thick and does not taste floury.

2. Whisk in the stock and cream until smooth. Bring the liquid to a boil. Season with salt and pepper to taste, but heavy on the black pepper is great for this sauce.

3. Remove from the heat and reserve. You will have extra velouté. Use it on everything from eggs Benedict (in place of hollandaise) to grilled steaks, fried chicken, or just a big bowl of mashed potatoes. It can be kept in the fridge for a few days and simply reheated on the stove in a sauté pan.

This simple, rich gravy made of chicken stock, roux, and cream is one of the four "mother sauces" of French cuisine. The word *velouté* is derived from the French adjective "velor" for velvety.

FINISHING IT OFF:

1. Break up the cheese curds into 1-inch pieces. Reheat the velouté sauce on the stove top to a slow simmer.

½ pound fresh cheese curds

Paper cups (thick enough for coffee, but no Styrofoam)

2. Place curds in 4 to 6 paper cups. Put hot fries in the cups to cover the cheese curds; fries should be sticking out of the cups. Finish each cup with a healthy dose of the velouté. Enjoy with a crisp, hoppy IPA, Lipitor, and Tums.

We use Calabro Mozzarella Curds, but mail-order Wisconsin curds are the best for this recipe; this requires some planning ahead but gives a great traditional squeaky quality to the dish when chewed.

duck sliders w. epoisse & dried figs

The term slider was coined by America's oldest fast-food chain, White Castle, in 1921. Today it is ubiquitously known as any small burger that can be taken down in less than a few bites. We love sliders because they are a fun way to pack as much flavor into a little burger as possible. Sliders are just plain fun, and duck breast is the perfect vehicle for them. Its richness would be too much in a large burger, especially with the addition of a big cheese like Epoisse. Adding peppery fresh arugula lifts up the savory cheese and duck, and the sweet dried black mission figs bring it all home.

FEEDS: 6

2 medium-size duck breasts

Kosher salt and freshly ground black pepper

¼ cup pure canola oil

6 slider rolls

½ small wheel, or approximately 6 ounces, Epoisse Berthaut

House mayonnaise (page 143)

6 small dried black mission figs, sliced in half

Handful of wild arugula (the spicier the better)

1. Preheat oven to 350°F.

2. Season the duck breasts generously with salt and pepper on both sides. Heat a medium-size pan with a few tablespoons of canola oil on high heat. Place the breasts fat side down in the pan and allow to cook for a few minutes until a deep brown crust forms on top of the stove. Place the whole pan in the preheated oven for an additional few minutes, cooking the duck to medium-rare.

3. Remove the duck from the oven and allow it to rest for a few minutes.

4. In the meantime, cut each roll in half and place on a baking sheet with a little bit of Epoisse on the top inside half of each roll. Toast in the preheated oven until cheese just starts to melt and rolls get slightly toasted.

5. Remove rolls from the oven and spread a little mayo on the sides that do not have cheese. Place a dried fig and some arugula on each roll.

6. Slice the duck breast on the bias as evenly as possible to get 6 slices per breast. Put 2 slices on each roll, and you are ready to eat.

LUPI LEGNA'S ITALIAN TABLE ROLLS

Located on Washington Avenue just around the corner from Yale New Haven Hospital, the old-style Marchigiano Bakery, Lupi Legna, has been in business in New Haven for over a century in the same location and with the same family. Larry Lupi's grandparents opened the business that he and his uncle Pete still run today. They make small Italian table rolls that, when cold, are flavorless and texturally bland, but when baked for a second time just before serving, transform into crusty light-crumbed wonders, perfect in size and flavor to hold sliders. Look for your local bakery—the longer it has been around, the better. Talk to them about what you need. Slider rolls should be crusty but not so hard that your filling comes flying out. Never settle for inferior bread when making a slider. When there are only a few bites to a dish, they must be perfect from top to bottom.

deep-fried sweetbreads w. artichokes, radicchio & lemon feta

The key to this recipe is the freshness of the ingredients. Using canned artichokes rather than fresh ones will make the dish feel flat and lacking. Take the time to trim the artichokes. Removing the brittle outer layer of leaves, peeling the stem, and coring out the prickly choke yields a tender, wonderful piece of vegetable that pairs perfectly with the bitter radicchio and rich, meaty sweetbreads. This dish is not easy and not quick, so why is it in the Smaller Plates section? Because it's awesome—not enough for a meal, but a fun challenge nonetheless. Take your time with the preparation and you'll see that this dish is worth the effort. Enjoy with a bright, minerally white wine such as a Muscadet. There is nothing "offal" about it!

FEEDS: 4

2 whole lemons

2 whole artichokes

1 head radicchio

½ cup fresh Sicilian extra-virgin olive oil

Kosher salt and freshly ground black pepper

1 pound sweetbreads (veal or lamb)

2 quarts peanut oil (for frying)

½ pound sheep's or goat's milk feta

Handful of flat-leaf parsley, coarsely chopped

Flour (for dredging)

8 cups milk

FOR THE ARTICHOKES AND RADICCHIO:

1. Cut one of the lemons in half and juice the halves into a bowl of cold water large enough to hold the artichokes.

2. Using a paring knife, work around the artichoke, removing the harder outer leaves until the tender baby leaves are revealed. Pull away the fibrous skin that covers the stem. Keep the stem intact—the stem is the most prized part of the artichoke.

3. Cut the artichoke in half and, with a teaspoon, dig away the spiny fibers of the choke. Now cut the halves into eighths and immediately get them into the lemon water.

4. Repeat the above steps for the second artichoke. Set aside, leaving in water until later.

5. Cut the radicchio into 8 even pieces. Toss in olive oil (a drizzled amount), salt, and pepper.

6. Place radicchio onto a parchment-lined baking sheet and place under the broiler set on high until caramelized. If you have a grill, it can be used for the caramelizing process as well. The radicchio should be nicely browned, but not burnt, on all sides of each piece. Set aside until later.

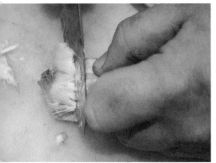

FOR THE SWEETBREADS:

1. Soak the sweetbreads in enough milk to cover them completely and change the milk every hour until they become whitish in color. You'll have to change the milk several times; this can take up to 5 hours.

2. Place the sweetbreads in a small saucepan and cover with cold salted water. Slowly bring the water up to a boil. As soon as it comes to a boil, remove, drain, and run breads under cold water.

3. Remove the skin and fibers, and cut the pieces into an approximately 1-inch size.

4. Place the sweetbreads on a sheet pan or pie plate between two paper towels and cover with a cutting board with a weight on top. Let the breads sit in the fridge for an hour to get as much moisture out as possible. This entire process can be done far in advance, 1 or 2 days, no more.

PREPARING THE FINISHED DISH:

1. Preheat 2 quarts of peanut oil to 375°F and put a 2-quart pot of water on to boil.

2. Combine the feta, cut into ½-inch cubes, olive oil, and juice and zest of the second lemon with some of the coarsely chopped parsley. Set aside for the finishing touches.

3. Blanch the prepared sweetbreads in boiling water, then dip immediately into ice water. Pat dry.

4. Pat the prepared artichoke hearts dry and fry in the peanut oil.

5. Dredge sweetbreads in flour seasoned with salt and pepper. Drop them into the preheated peanut oil, being sure not to crowd them too much in the pan. Fry in batches if necessary.

6. Pat the prepared artichoke hearts dry and fry in the peanut oil.

7. Place the sweetbreads, artichokes, and warm broiled/grilled radicchio on a plate or in a bowl lined with a brown paper bag. I like to sprinkle on extra salt and pepper just before serving as well. Top the entire thing off with the lemoned feta just before serving or as an accompaniment. Now enjoy your thymus glands!

leek & goat cheese tart

This tart has been on our menu from day one and is by far one of our most popular dishes. Each day Steve goes into the cheese shop and asks Lydia or Sylvia what he should use in the tart. He tells them he has broccoli or shallots or simply a big bunch of fresh herbs from the rooftop, and they suggest a wedge of this or hunk of that. The version below is straight-up classic and one of my favorites, but play with as many combinations as you can.

MAKES 6 TARTS

2 cups flour plus more for bench flour

Pinch of salt

½ pound unsalted butter cubed and ice cold from the fridge

Approximately a ⅓-cup ice cold water

FOR THE PÂTE BRISÉE:

1. Combine flour, salt, and unsalted butter in the bowl of an electric mixer with a paddle attachment. Mix until the unsalted butter is crumbled into small pieces, about the size of peas. Slowly add only enough water to make the dough come together.

2. Remove the dough and gently roll into a ball then flatten like a pancake to about 1 inch thick. Wrap the dough in plastic film and let rest in the refrigerator for 20 minutes.

3. Remove the dough from the fridge and allow it to come to room temperature, about 15 minutes or so.

4. Roll out pâte brisée dough to about ¼ inch thick. Use some bench flour to keep it from sticking.

5. Cut circles in the rolled-out dough to form individual tart rings and place on a baking sheet. Or, using a paring knife, cut small disks in the dough and place in greased cupcake tins.

4 leeks (white and light green parts only)

2 tablespoons unsalted butter

Kosher salt and freshly ground black pepper

FOR THE FILLING:

1. Preheat oven to 425° F.

2. Wash and cut leeks into small pieces. Allow leeks to float in a bowl of water for a few minutes. Rinse them again to remove all sand and dirt.

3. Heat unsalted butter in a sauté pan over medium heat until it begins to foam. Lightly sauté leeks until tender and fragrant. Season to taste with salt and pepper.

4. Remove to a clean bowl and let cool.

FOR THE CUSTARD:

1. Whisk the cream and the eggs together. Season with a pinch of salt and some freshly ground black pepper.

2. Into each uncooked tart shell evenly divide a little piece of the cheese and some of the sautéed leeks. Here you can put as little or as much as you see fit.

This is more custard than you'll need for your tarts, but extra custard is NOT a bad thing!

PREPARING THE TARTS:

1. Add the custard, enough to come to ¼ inch from the top of the tart shell.

2. Brush the tart shell with the egg wash.

3. Bake for 30–40 minutes or until golden brown and the custard has just gently set. You want the custard to be still jiggly when you take out the tarts and they will carry over cooking out of the oven. Serve warm or at room temperature or even the next day reheated.

2 cups cream

3 whole eggs

Pinch Kosher salt and freshly ground black pepper

8–10 ounces goat cheese/chèvre, crumbled

Egg wash (1 egg mixed with 1 tablespoon milk)

steve vandroff

TITLE: Pastry Chef, Sous Chef, Tart King, champion of the pot d'crème

BIRTHPLACE: Brooklyn, New York

HOBBIES: Florida Gators football and Syracuse Orangemen basketball fan, sports video-game expert, drawing, collecting sports memorabilia, watching movies, and enjoying long walks to the train station.

FAVORITE DISH TO MAKE AT HOME: My favorite meal includes potato salad, corn bread, collards, fried chicken or ribs, and homemade ice tea (sweet tea like Mom makes every time I go down south to see her).

SPECIALTY IN THE KITCHEN: Pâte brisée dough, tarts, desserts, the Chocolate Pot d'Crème.

WHAT DO YOU LOVE ABOUT CASEUS? I love the atmosphere, the employees—all of it. I love my job. I tell people all the time—I really love my job!

lamb sliders w. neal's yard dairy colston bassett stilton & pea shoots

What the hell is a pea shoot? It's the young, first few inches of a pea vine, also known as a pea tendril. These little spring sprigs deliver a concentrated burst of vegetal freshness. They're historically based in Asian cuisine and typically served wok-fried with fish. In recent years they have become a hot addition to salads, sandwiches, and garnishes in the United States and Europe. They are easiest to find at your local farmers' market and can run anywhere from $6 to $12 per pound. Pricey, but well worth it, and a little goes a long way.

FEEDS: 6 AS A SNACK OR 2 FOR A SERIOUS MEAL!

1 pound organic ground lamb (American lamb, usually from Colorado, is best)

2 teaspoons chopped cured lemons (page 138)

2 large shallots, finely diced

1 clove garlic, very finely diced

Kosher salt and freshly ground black pepper

1 tablespoon fresh, local unsalted butter

6 slider rolls

House mayonnaise (page 143)

⅔ pound Neal's Yard Dairy Colston Bassett Stilton

Healthy pinch of pea shoots

1. Preheat oven to 350°F.

2. Combine the ground lamb, cured lemons, shallots, garlic, and a healthy pinch of kosher salt and pepper. Form 6 patties of equal size. Set aside in the fridge to rest momentarily.

3. In a medium-size sauté pan, heat the butter until foaming. Season the outside top and bottom of each patty with salt and pepper and place in the pan with the butter. Brown the patties on both sides and place in the preheated oven.

4. Slice the slider rolls in half and toast in the oven with the lamb patties, until golden brown and crisp.

5. Remove the toasted rolls and spread a little mayo on the bottom half of each roll.

6. Put a little bit of the Stilton on each patty during the last minute of cooking to just slightly melt the cheese. Be sure to remove after 1 minute; you don't want the cheese to melt too much.

7. Finish the sliders by putting them on the toasted rolls with mayo, and topping each Stilton-adorned patty with a pinch of pea shoots before capping them with the roll tops.

8. Serve immediately with a dark beer, such as Samuel Smith's Oatmeal Stout.

NEAL'S YARD DAIRY COLSTON BASSETT STILTON

Made in the same tradition since 1920, this is the all-time best, top-of-the-line, number-one Stilton on the planet. It is made from five nearby farms' pristine cow's milk using animal rennet for a seriously creamy taste, not necessarily pungent or sweet but just straddling the line between spicy and piquant. If you make this recipe, use this cheese; if you can't find it, call me. My number at Caseus is (203) 624-3373.

If you really can't find this amazing Stilton, I guess you could try looking for a similar blue cheese with a creamy texture but still-assertive blue flavor. Roquefort works, as well as Bayley Hazen Blue from Jasper Hill Farm in Vermont.

bread & butter

Such a simple concept done right can be superbly soul-satisfying. This has been a surprisingly popular dish for us. At first we got a ton of flack from customers angry about being charged $4 for bread and butter. But once we explained that the butter was made daily with fresh fruits and spices and the bread was slowly fermented and brought in from specialty bakeries, customers began to take interest. After they tried the dish, the response was positive. We gladly provide simple baguettes and plain unsalted butter upon request at no charge.

FRENCH TOAST BUTTER

1 pound good, fresh, local unsalted butter

1 cup local maple syrup (or your favorite real maple syrup)

1 tablespoon kosher salt or Maldon salt

1 tablespoon good cinnamon

1 teaspoon ground ginger

1. Allow the butter to sit out and come to room temperature.

2. Cut the butter into 1-inch cubes and place in a food processor or upright mixer with the paddle attachment. Whip the butter and, once nice and smooth, add the rest of the ingredients.

3. Put the butter in a large bowl, or place the butter on a large sheet of parchment paper and, using the paper, roll into a log. Allow to rest in the fridge until chilled and all the flavors have nicely combined.

We get the bulk of our maple syrup from a gentleman named Lindsey who has a small sugar shack in North Branford (two towns down the road from Caseus). He trades his syrup for dinners with his wife. The syrup is thinner and darker than conventional syrup and has a rich maple flavor with a bit less sweetness.

Maldon salt is a flakey, delicious English sea salt.

PEACH & BASIL BUTTER

1 pound good, fresh, local unsalted butter

1 cup lightly packed basil leaves

2 large ripe peaches

2 tablespoons good local honey

1 teaspoon kosher salt or Maldon salt

1 teaspoon freshly ground black pepper

1. Cut the butter into 1-inch cubes and allow to sit out until soft but not melted.

2. Bring a small pot of water to a boil, and prepare a small bowl of ice water next to it. Once the water comes to a heavy roll, drop the basil in for 10 seconds.

3. Remove the basil with a strainer and place into the ice water. Keep the water boiling.

4. Cut a cross on the top of each peach and drop into the same boiling water. Allow the peaches to poach in the water for about 2 minutes. Transfer the peaches into the same ice water that the basil is shocking in.

5. Remove the peaches from the water. Remove the skins and pits from each peach and dice into ¼-inch pieces.

6. Drain the basil as thoroughly as possible, patting it dry and squeezing it out with a kitchen towel. Chop the basil finely and combine with the chopped peaches.

7. Combine the softened butter, peaches and basil, honey, salt, and pepper in a large bowl using a wooden spoon. Mix the ingredients until combined well but not a mashed mess.

8. Tightly pack the butter into a small bowl, or place the butter on a large piece of parchment paper and, using the paper, roll into a log. Allow to sit overnight in the fridge so that the flavors combine.

OTHER COMBINATIONS WE LOVE:

Strawberry and black pepper
Honey and sea salt
Boquerones and lemon zest
Roasted pepper and kalamata olive

Look to serve breads made using a slow fermentation process. Fruit- and nut-studded breads, sourdough boules, ficelles, and baguettes work well. Always serve your bread lightly toasted and warm. This allows the cold butter to melt on the hot bread, truly one of life's greatest pleasures.

Caseus Tomato Soup, 30

Zucchini Soup w. Crème Fraîche, 31

Roasted Crimini Mushroom Soup w. Mascarpone, 32

Chicken & Corn Chowda, 34

Joe's Escarole & Beans w. Piacentinu Ennese, 36

Cassoulet the Caseus Way, 38

New England Clam Chowda, 40

Vegan Black Bean Soup, 42

French Onion Soup, 44

SOUPS, STEWS & CHOWDAS

Nothing beats a cool, velvety, smooth soup on a hot summer day. Conversely, the warmth of a hearty winter soup chock-full of slow-cooked vegetables heats up both the bones and the most inner reaches of the soul. At Caseus, we always have French Onion Soup. It's a staple, and because of its cheesy component, the dish fits us perfectly. We also make a simple vegetarian soup du jour, and this section includes some of our most popular and requested soups. Variations are easily made, as well as fusion soups, where we combine two or three soups. During the winter and fall seasons, we also do stews and chowdas. Our cassoulet is said to have magical powers, and our chicken corn chowda is rivaled by nothing in the universe. As a starter, meal, or even dessert, soups are a great way to incorporate a soft-textured delivery of flavor to all parts of the mouth while somehow always satisfying the soul.

caseus tomato soup

At Caseus, seasonality is key. If you ask for a slice of tomato with your cheeseburger in January, you're not going to get it. We don't have any tomatoes but for a few months in the summer when we can get heirloom varieties locally grown and picked fresh from the vine. But we do need to have tomato soup for our Grilled Cheese, so we use high-quality, basic canned tomatoes with only a few other ingredients. The result is a simple, delightful soup that warms the soul and fills the belly.

FEEDS: 4–6

2 tablespoons pure canola oil

Do not substitute olive oil, as the onions may burn.

2 large Spanish onions, thinly sliced

6 cloves fresh garlic, peeled and crushed with the side of a knife

1 cup good dry white wine

3 28-ounce cans peeled, crushed, all-natural tomatoes

Check to make sure there are only tomatoes in the can, no salt or other preservatives added.

¾ cup heavy cream

Use as local and as fresh as you can get.

½ cup unsalted butter

We use Cabot unsalted butter from Vermont.

Kosher salt and freshly ground black pepper

1. Put the canola oil in a large lidded pot and heat slowly over medium heat. Add the onions and allow them to caramelize. Do this with the pot lid on. You are looking to lightly brown the onions but not get them very dark.

2. When the onions are soft and lightly browned, add the garlic. Once the garlic becomes soft, deglaze the pot with the white wine, scraping up any fond from the pot's surface. Let the wine reduce slightly until you cannot taste the alcohol. Watch it at this point, as it's apt to burn here.

3. Add the tomatoes and allow the liquid to come up to a simmer.

4. Remove in batches into a blender and blend on high (carefully, as this will be hot!). Return to the pot when velvety smooth and allow to simmer on low for as long as possible or up to a couple hours. If possible, make this a day ahead and refrigerate to maximize flavor.

5. When ready to serve, heat the soup slowly and add cream and butter until just incorporated. DO NOT BOIL! Add salt and pepper to taste. Serve with Caseus Grilled Cheese sandwiches (page 86).

zucchini soup w. crème fraîche

Zucchini is one of those vegetables that's readily available year-round. But the ones you get from your local farmers' market, picked hours before you buy them, yield the best soups. This soup can be made with yellow summer squash as well, but again the key is to get good, fresh squash. Cook it as soon as you can to retain the bright squashy flavors and take advantage of all the healthy nutrients that go hand-in-hand with fresh-picked vegetables. Be sure to douse the whole mess with a big dollop of good crème fraîche. We get ours from Vermont Butter and Creamery.

FEEDS: 4–6

1. Preheat oven to 400°F.

2. Cut the zucchini into even rounds, about ½-inch thick, and place on two parchment-lined baking sheets. Put them in the oven dry—no seasoning and no oil—for about 10–15 minutes. Watch them; you don't want them to burn. The idea is that you are concentrating them and removing some of their moisture.

3. While the zucchini roasts in the oven, put the canola oil and onions in a large lidded pot over medium heat and allow the onions to slowly caramelize. Be sure not to let them get dark brown, only golden.

4. When the onions are soft and lightly browned, add the garlic. Once the garlic becomes soft, deglaze the pot with the white wine, scraping up any fond from the pot's surface. Let the wine reduce slightly until you cannot taste alcohol.

5. Add the roasted zucchini from the oven and top, by about 2 inches, everything with water or some nice chicken stock (page 139). You choose how much liquid to add here, as some like their soups thicker and others thinner.

6. Allow this to gently simmer for at least an hour and then let sit for another hour to come down in temperature.

7. Remove in batches into a blender and blend on high (carefully!). Taste and season with salt and pepper. Return to the pot when smooth and allow to simmer on low for at least a half hour to slowly reduce. If possible, make this a day ahead and refrigerate for 24 hours to maximize flavor.

8. When ready to serve (either hot or cold), top each bowl with a nice dollop of cool crème fraîche and a pinch of fresh chopped chervil, basil, or cilantro. Serve with toasted baguettes smeared with fresh chèvre and lightly broiled.

5 or 6 medium fresh zucchini

2 tablespoons pure canola oil

Do not substitute olive oil, as the onions may burn.

2 large Spanish onions, thinly sliced

6 cloves fresh garlic, peeled and crushed with the side of a knife

1 cup good dry white wine

Kosher salt and freshly ground black pepper

Vermont Butter and Creamery crème fraîche, or your favorite brand

Handful of chopped chervil, basil, or cilantro (optional)

Look similar to the Caseus Tomato Soup recipe? It is—this method makes great simple soups.

Mint is a wonderful addition to this soup as well and works perfectly if you serve this soup chilled rather than hot in the summer.

roasted crimini mushroom soup w. mascarpone

Typically we'll use shitakes, chanterelles, morels (when we're really lucky), and lots of hen of the woods mushrooms to highlight a special entree on any given night. We'll save the stems and any tired-looking specialty mushrooms to make a banging mushroom stock for our mushroom soups. But at home this simple soup can be made with tap water, and the dish comes out wonderfully creamy and robust with just crimini mushrooms, whose flavor is brought out by a quick roast in a hot oven. Paired with an earthy and oniony Swiss cheese like Scharfer Maxx, this soup is the perfect simple go-to for any meal.

FEEDS: 4–6

3 pounds crimini mushrooms

4 tablespoons good canola oil

7 or 8 sprigs fresh thyme

Kosher salt and freshly ground black pepper

2 tablespoons pure canola oil

Do not substitute olive oil, as the onions may burn.

2 large Spanish onions, thinly sliced

4 cloves fresh garlic, peeled and crushed with the side of a knife

2 cups tawny port

The general rule is this: If you wouldn't drink it, don't cook with it.

½ pound shredded Scharfer Maxx cheese or any Alpine cheese with a strong, oniony flavor such as Gruyère or Wildspitz

1. Preheat oven to 400°F.

2. Toss mushrooms in canola oil, thyme (removed from the stems), salt, and pepper. Coat evenly. Spread the mushrooms out on a parchment-lined sheet pan and place in the oven for about 10 minutes to roast.

3. Meanwhile, in a large soup pot over medium heat, combine the canola oil and onions. Sweat in the pot until the onions are translucent and slightly caramelized then add the garlic. Deglaze the pot with the port. Allow to reduce over high heat, scrapping the bottom of the pan, for a few minutes.

4. Add the roasted mushrooms; be sure not to let any large rogue thyme stems get into the pot. Cover everything with water and allow the soup to come to a boil, then simmer for about an hour.

5. Let cool slightly and carefully transfer into a blender in small batches. Blend until mixture is velvety smooth. Season to taste, adding lots of freshly ground black pepper. Allow to sit overnight to marry the flavors, if possible.

6. When ready to serve, grate the cheese in large ribbons with a vegetable peeler and top each soup just as you're serving it. Serve with crusty bread and a salad dressed with bright sherry vinaigrette (see recipe page 144), or just hunks of the cheese and bread on the side.

This soup works well served cold or hot, but my favorite thing to do with it is to mix it with a little Madeira or port and use it as a sauce for meats. Crepes drizzled with this are also ridiculously awesome.

chicken & corn chowda

Corn is definitely one of our favorite things to eat. Thursday is corn night at Caseus in the summer, when locally grown varieties are abundant. A simple grilled corn on the cob barely heated through can be one of the most satisfying experiences ever. Be sure you know who has grown your corn and when it has been picked. Get it into your mouth as soon as you can after it's been taken from the stalk. Corn's sugars turn to starch the longer it's away from the stalk, so only buy what you'll eat at one sitting. Then drive out to the farm stand the next day for a few more ears.

FEEDS: 8–10

1 bulb fresh fennel with the fronds

About 1 8-ounce log of good, fresh, local chèvre

We use chèvre from Beltane Farm in Lebanon, Connecticut.

10 ears fresh corn

2 large russet potatoes, cut into ¼-inch dice; leave the peels on for more flavor!

2 medium red onions

2 small shallots

3 cloves garlic

½ cup fresh, local unsalted butter

Kosher salt and freshly ground black pepper

1 tablespoon all-purpose (AP) flour

3 cups whole milk

1 roast chicken (page 92), meat picked from the carcass

It's as little or as much meat as you'd like to add. Rabbit, duck, or turkey would work too. Or something thick-cut so you can make nice chunky lardons.

½ pound slab bacon

1 bunch fresh chives

1. Cut the fennel fronds off of the bulb and give them a good rough chop. You'll use the bulb later, so don't chuck it.

2. In a stand mixer with a paddle attachment, mix the chèvre with the fennel fronds. Don't overmix—just get the fronds evenly incorporated. Roll the fennel chèvre into a nice log, using parchment or plastic wrap, and put it in the fridge. This can be done a day or so ahead.

3. Remove all of the husks and silk from the ears of corn. Carefully cut the corn kernels off of the ears and put them into a bowl to be used later.

4. Put the corn cobs, now bare of kernels, into a large pot. If necessary, cut them in half so that they all fit. Add about 10 cups of water, or just enough to cover the corn cobs. Bring to a boil and allow to simmer for about an hour.

5. Remove the cobs from the now-finished corn stock and discard. Add the corn kernels and the diced potatoes to the stock. Let simmer another 15 minutes, or until the potatoes are tender but still slightly firm.

6. Cut onions, shallots, garlic, and fennel into a small dice and add to a deep, heavy-bottomed stock pot with the butter. Sweat over medium heat until the ingredients are nicely translucent. Season well with salt and pepper.

7. Add the flour, evenly stirring it into the onion mixture so it coats well. Stir and cook for a little longer to get the flour nicely toasted.

8. Turn off the heat. With the heat off, add the milk and stir until it's nicely incorporated.

9. Add the corn stock, potato, and corn mixture to the pot with the onions, shallots, garlic, fennel, and milk until combined. Hold off adding too much of the corn stock liquid if you desire a thicker chowda.

TO COMPLETE THE SOUP:

1. Add the picked, cooked leftover chicken meat. Let the soup sit for at least an hour, or refrigerate overnight to serve the next day.

2. Before serving the soup, render off the bacon lardons until nicely crisp and a deep, dark, fatty brown.

3. Gently heat the soup, being sure not to bring it to a boil. Serve each bowl of chowda topped with the crisp hot bacon, a good bit of chopped chives, and a nice blob of the fennel frond chèvre.

jœ's escarole & beans w. piacentinu ennese

During the Norman occupation of Sicily in the late fourteenth century, one of the Norman leaders held a competition in search of a cure to his many wives' woes. Turns out, he needed a way to get his wives a bit more interested in him in the bedroom. The winning solution was a sheep's milk cheese, Piacentinu Ennese, made with Sicilian saffron and whole black peppercorns. Both sweet and acidic, with a nuttiness from the saffron and peppercorn, this cheese packs in the flavor and can even persuade throngs of damsels to sleep with old, lecherous Norman invaders! Can't find this cheese? Use another bright, young pecorino instead. Sardinian Bianco Sardo or even a nice raw-milk Spanish Manchego works great.

FEEDS: 4–6

1 pound dried cannelini beans

1 large Spanish onion

½ cup unsalted butter

3 cloves fresh garlic

5 cups chicken stock (page 139)

2 large organic carrots

2 heads clean escarole

Kosher salt and freshly ground black pepper

1 stale baguette of the highest quality

¾ pound Piacentinu Ennese, grated on the large holes of a box grater

1 bunch flat-leaf parsley, coarsely chopped

Great extra-virgin olive oil for drizzlin'

We've found that blanching the escarole in the soup broth and then shocking it makes it hold a more toothsome texture and brings out the sweetness in the greens. It's a little more work, but well worth the effort.

1. Rinse the beans really well, and make sure there are no little stones. The night before you make this soup, soak the beans in enough water so that they are covered by three of your fingers (three fingers of water over the beans). In the morning your beans will probably have soaked up a good amount of the water, if not all of it. This makes them much easier to digest. (You're not going to fart as much!)

2. Cut the onions into a large dice. Place them in a soup pot with the unsalted butter and sauté over medium heat. Add the garlic cloves whole and continue to sauté for a little longer until the onions are nice and translucent.

3. Add the chicken stock (or if you prefer, vegetable stock) and the soaked beans. Cook gently until the beans are tender; this may take up to a half hour or more. The beans will slightly thicken the soup, but you can add water as you need it.

4. Once the beans are nicely cooked, add the carrots cut into large, rustic rounds. They should be nice and firm and left unpeeled.
Less effort in peeling them, and more nutrients in eating them.

5. Cut the escarole into large strips (be sure it's properly cleaned and rinsed). Blanch the escarole in the soup. To do this, get the soup nice and hot (but not yet boiling), drop the escarole into the soup, and let it wilt completely. Then, with tongs or a spider, scoop the escarole out and into a bowl of ice water. Let it cool completely; it will stay firm and bright, and its bitterness will be quelled as well. Take the escarole out of the water, draining it, and put it aside for serving.

6. Adjust the soup with salt and lots of fresh cracked pepper. Don't make it too salty, because you're going to add a bunch of cheese at the end.

7. To serve, place a little of the blanched escarole in each bowl, followed by a few large hunks of the stale baguette, and then top with the brothy bean and carrot soup. Finish with a good handful of grated cheese, some fresh parsley, and a drizzle of great extra-virgin olive oil. This soup is wonderful in the wintertime, and is best eaten simply with a glass of hearty red wine. I like to add a nice piece of leftover sausage or chicken last-minute with the escarole as well—boom!

joe

TITLE: Chef, aka Yo-Yo

BIRTHPLACE: Bridgeport, Connecticut

HOBBIES: Eating; collecting old Bell Atlantic trucks, cars, and motorcycles; comic books; listening to music; and attending concerts.

FAVORITE DISH TO MAKE AT HOME: Peasant food, stews with grilled bread and cheese, ribollita.

WHAT DO YOU LOVE ABOUT CASEUS? My regulars. The family atmosphere. I grew up with the owner, he's an old friend. I love the guys in the kitchen, the crew. I love my freedom in the kitchen with the creation of the dishes.

FAVORITE CASEUS MEAL? Short ribs or the osso bucco. I love the braising dishes. I love the scallops in the summer (for the first month, and then I get sick of them!). It's tough keeping over a hundred pounds of heirloom tomatoes in stock at a time!

cassoulet the caseus way

Cassoulet is the ultimate French comfort food. Beans, sausage, confit duck—all cooked together in a rich stew for a long period of time. There have to be more recipes for cassoulet out there than people willing to make it! Our version is certainly simpler than the traditional French version but by no means is it a "30-minute meal," so carve out some time for this dish—you will be rewarded.

Once you've made the duck confit, the rest of the cassoulet is pretty easy. Never make your cassoulet the same way twice. Consistency is better left to McDonald's and TGI Friday's than to cooks who use what's immediate and situational. The most important aspect to cooking cassoulet is to have fun.

FEEDS: AS MANY AS YOU'D LIKE

This recipe is more an idea or a feeling. The lack of measurements and time are intentional so that you truly make this the Caseus way—that is, different each time but yielding the same result, which is a supremely comforting stew loaded with beans, duck, and sausage.

Cassoulet should be made in large batches and consumed over the course of several days. You'll find yourself making rice one night and then egg noodles the next to serve alongside it. Don't be shy about throwing a nice sunny-side-up fried egg atop a leftover portion of cassoulet for breakfast either. That is one serious way to start your day.

TO MAKE CASSOULET, THE CASEUS WAY:

LAMB MERGUEZ SAUSAGE: This is best purchased from a reputable butcher. We use Fabrique Delice, a charcuterie in San Francisco that uses all-natural meats in its products. Merguez sausage is originally Algerian. It is made from lamb and beef, and has harissa (a red chili paste), among other spices, stuffed into lamb casings. It is one of my favorites!

GOOD SLAB BACON: Don't get store-bought sliced bacon. You need to have big chunks for this recipe. Try 1 x 1-inch squares. If you can't find slab bacon, ask your butcher for a piece of pork belly, skin on. That'll do just fine.

GARLIC: Peeled cloves—lots and lots of them!

CARROTS, ONIONS, CELERY, AND FENNEL: Rough chopped.

ANY SCRAPS YOU HAVE KICKING AROUND: Mushrooms, bell peppers, squash, butt ends of prosciutto, miscellaneous nubs of dried sausages . . . pretty much anything.

VEAL STOCK: This is crucial and a must-have.

BEEF STOCK: This is necessary but not crucial.

LAMB STOCK: This is great but not necessary.

BEANS: Opinions differ, but I prefer navy beans (never canned). Get them dried and soak them overnight.

DUCK CONFIT: Lots of it! (page 66)

A BOTTLE, OR TWO, OF DECENT LEFTOVER WINE

FRESH THYME, MARJORAM, AND ROSEMARY: Be liberal!

1. Preheat oven to 350ish°F.

2. In a large, heavy-bottomed, oven-safe pot (preferably an enameled cast-iron Dutch oven) render off the sausages and bacon lightly.

3. Once they've released some of their fat into the pot, add the garlic, carrots, onions, celery, and fennel. Any scraps you have can be added now as well. Let cook until a bit of color is left on the vegetables and they get just ever so slightly translucent but not at all soft, about 7 minutes.

4. Add the veal stock and any other stock you have to cover the mixture, and add the soaked beans as well.

5. Here you can now add the duck confit. Shred it from the bones and toss the shredded duck into the pot. Be sure to toss in the skin too.

6. Add the wine and the fresh herbs, and cover it all. Bring to a boil on top of the stove.

7. Now put the entire pot into the preheated oven to cook for about 4 hours or so. Every hour you must take it out, give it a stir, and decide if you need to add a bit of water or stock to the mix. The beans will, of course, soak up a good bit of the liquid, so if it looks dry, add liquid.

8. Serve with a hearty red wine and some crusty bread with a bit of strong cheese melted on top; we love to use robust, oniony Swiss cheeses like Napf to stand up to the big stew. Dress some arugula with lemon juice and extra-virgin olive oil, and you've put together just about the most complete meal known to man.

new england clam chowda

The morning after a hazy night partying in college, my roommates told me that I had recited in detail the difference between New England, Rhode Island, and Manhattan clam chowders. I don't recall doing this, but I do know that when it comes to Clam Chowda, New England is the only way to go. Nothing thick and snotty, but a nice robust broth with a hint of cream complements the clams to no end. For ease of operation, if you must use canned clams, I understand. But there is nothing more delicate and wonderful than fresh littlenecks pulled from the New England seas. My grandfather-in-law, Louie, goes out to dig them up from the sands of Long Island Sound every morning. They are pretty tasty when simply pried open and hit with lemon juice and Tabasco. When Louie has extra, and he always does, this dish is one of my favorite ways to cook them up.

FEEDS: 8–10

40 or so littleneck or topneck clams, or 1 quart canned chopped clams

½ pound slab bacon

Or something thick-cut so you can make nice chunky lardons.

2 medium white onions

2 small shallots

3 cloves garlic

5 good, clean celery stalks, leaves on

1 carrot

2 large russet potatoes, cut into ¼-inch dice; leave the peels on for more flavor!

1 8-ounce bottle clam broth

3 cups whole milk

Kosher salt and freshly ground black pepper

1 cup cream

Beltane Farm's Herbes de Provence chèvre log; if you can't find this then roll a plain log of good chèvre in Herbs de Provence and now you've got it!

1 bunch fresh chives

¼ cup Pedro Ximenez sherry

1. Scrub the clams, discarding any that are not tightly closed.

2. Bring a few quarts of water up to a hard boil in a deep stock pot. Add the cleaned clams and cover. Stir them once and keep an eye on them so that they cook until just opened.

3. Remove the clams from the pot and shuck and chop them coarsely; if any are unopened then they are sadly destined for the trash. Set them aside in a bowl for later. Run the water from the pot through a sieve with cheesecloth to get rid of any leftover sand, and hold the stock in a small bowl for later.

4. In another large pot, add the bacon, cut into nice lardons, and begin to render off the fat. Once some fat has come out and it has gotten nicely crisp and brown, add the onions, shallots, garlic, celery, and carrot, all coarsely diced. Allow to cook until nicely soft but not mushy.

5. Add the potatoes, reserved clam stock, clam broth, and milk. Let simmer very gently for about 10 minutes. Taste and adjust seasoning with salt and pepper.

6. Add the cream and the clams and stir to incorporate. DO NOT BOIL! Just gently heat through and taste for seasoning. The less time the chopped clams sit in the hot soup, the better, as they can get tough. If you plan on serving this chowda the next day (I suggest it), let the base cool down slightly, then add the cream and clams and let cool completely before refrigerating overnight.

7. When you are ready to serve, heat the soup slowly and gently on the stove. Garnish each bowl with a nice medallion slice of the Beltane Herbes de Provence chèvre, some fresh chopped chives, and a splash of sherry.

More bacon on top is never a bad thing!

This recipe is made for the Fourth of July, enjoyed out of a paper coffee cup. Be sure to use the best clams and bacon you can find. Now sip your Sea Hag and marvel at the fireworks while you listen to the New England Sound lap at your toes.

There is no better beverage to enjoy with a bangin' New England Clam Chowda than a fresh, hoppy IPA. New England Brewery in Woodbridge, right down the road from us, makes Sea Hag. In my not-so-humble opinion, it is one of the finest IPAs on the market.

vegan black bean soup

Our vegetarian soups will typically have some cream, and most always contain a nice amount of fresh Vermont unsalted butter. But this soup is vegan, no dairy at all! Yet it's a damn fine soup. And it's easy to make and extremely satisfying in both the warmer and cooler months.

FEEDS: 4–6

2 large Spanish onions

2 large carrots

3 big, long celery stalks, leaves on

2 tablespoons good extra-virgin olive oil

3 cloves fresh garlic

Kosher salt and freshly ground black pepper

1 tablespoon dried whole cumin

1 teaspoon dried whole coriander

1 bay leaf

1 pound dried black beans

1 jalapeño pepper

1 bunch washed and dried cilantro

Pinch of cayenne pepper

Fresh limes for garnish

Bunch chives, parsley, or cilantro for garnish

1. Cut the onions, carrots, and celery into a large dice (about 1 inch plus) and toss into a large, heavy-bottomed soup or stock pot with the olive oil. Heat over medium heat. Throw in the whole garlic cloves once the onions start to turn translucent. Add a pinch of salt and some good grinds of fresh pepper.

2. Toast the cumin and coriander in a dry pan over low heat until fragrant. Transfer to a spice grinder or coffee grinder and grind until fine. Add to the cooking vegetables.

3. Cover vegetables with about 4–5 quarts of water and add a bay leaf. Bring to a gentle boil. Add the dried black beans (be sure to rinse the beans really well, and make sure there are no little stones) and let simmer until beans are tender. This can take up to an hour or more. Keep a watch and stir frequently.

4. Once the beans are cooked, fish out the bay leaf and discard. Add the jalapeño, cut into a small dice with seeds and ribs removed, and some fresh cilantro, coarsely chopped. Use as little or as much as you like of these two ingredients for heat and that unique cilantro taste some people love and others hate.

5. Taste and adjust with salt, ground black pepper, and a pinch (or more if you like) of cayenne pepper.

6. Allow soup to cool slightly. Transfer in small batches to a blender and blend on high until nicely emulsified. This extra time in the blender produces a creaminess in the soup that fools you into thinking it's got some cream or butter in it. It is worth the extra time it takes.

7. Let rest overnight in the refrigerator. This soup truly benefits from a night to rest before serving. Making it one or two days ahead melds all of its simple flavors together for one seriously wonderful yet basic soup.

8. To serve, garnish with a wedge of fresh lime and some fresh chives, coarsely chopped parsley, or cilantro. Enjoy with charcoal-grilled skirt steaks served bloody rare with a mojo sauce and a big, refreshing, cold beer like Pacifico, with some Tabasco splashed into it. For a unique variation, try this soup chilled with a nice dollop of crème fraîche spiked with cilantro or chilies.

french onion soup

This dish is simply an excuse to melt cheese. Here we have the most classic of all classic dishes: French Onion Soup. We sell this like mad in the winter and fall, but since it's on our menu as a staple year-round, it's not uncommon to see the lone diehard basking in the ripping hot sun of July, lifting up large ribbons of molten cheese over his head and into his mouth. Personally, I don't touch the stuff until the temperature drops below forty.

FEEDS: 4

7 large Spanish onions

3 tablespoons fresh unsalted butter

3 cloves fresh garlic

¼ cup tawny port

Use the cheap stuff and you'll not be happy, so pony up for something decent.

1 bay leaf

10 sprigs fresh thyme

½ bottle good, robust red wine

Something dry and Spanish and leftover is perfect.

2 quarts beef stock (page 140); the recipe we have will need to be doubled!

Kosher salt and freshly ground black pepper

Sourdough ficelle or old baguette, sliced and preferably stale

½ cup plus of cheese per portion of soup

We use a blend of Raclette, Gruyère, Comté, Provolone, and 2-year-aged Gouda.

1. Peel and cut the onions into thin ribbons, but not too thin (about ⅛ inch or so). I like to cut them up into several sizes so that some of the onions melt away while others stay toothsome.

2. Over medium heat, warm the butter in a large stock pot or, for best results, in a thick, enameled cast-iron Dutch oven. Allow the butter to begin to melt, and then add all of the onions at once. It's a ton of onions, but they will sweat down considerably. If need be, cook them in two batches. Cook the onions uncovered and check them every so often, using a wooden spoon to stir them around so that the ones on top get some bottom time.

3. Meanwhile, peel the garlic cloves, smack them with a knife, and throw them into the pot with the onions. They should not be minced but merely slightly flattened.

   The smaller the garlic is cut, the more forceful its flavor. By keeping it whole but simply smacked you release some of its sweetness but none of the spicy robustness that garlic can incorporate.

4. After about 30–45 minutes, the onions should be a nice golden to dark brown color and soft and translucent.

5. Pour the port into the pot with the onions and, using your wooden spoon, scrape/deglaze the bottom of the pot as much as you can. Be sure to get the sides and edges so that entire bottom of the pot is now clean.

6. Add the bay leaf, thyme, red wine, and beef stock. Season with salt and pepper until desired flavor is achieved, but don't go too heavy on the salt. As you cook the soup, it will reduce and intensify in flavor.

7. Let all of this simmer lightly on the stove for at least 4 hours (preferably longer) and—this is very important—allow to cool and store overnight to be reheated the next day.

When done right, this is the most wonderfully satisfying dish around. Once a guy came into the restaurant and asked for a raw egg in the shell with his French Onion Soup. When it came to the table, he dug out a nice little hole through the thick cheese layer on top of the bowl and cracked the egg into it. He let it sit for a minute and then dug in. The heat of the soup cooked the egg and made what is already one of our richer dishes seriously over the top.

THE FOLLOWING DAY:

1. Slowly reheat the soup on the stove top. Meanwhile, preheat the broiler in the oven.

2. Set out 4 oven-safe onion soup crocks. (These can be purchased at your local restaurant supply store.) Onion soup crocks are fat and bulbous in the middle and come to a nice, slightly smaller, round top, allowing you to load your cheese and bread on top but not overwhelm the brothy, oniony goodness.

3. Fill each crock with soup, then top with a piece of sliced stale bread and some shredded cheese. Place the crocks in the oven with the broiler cranking.

DO NOT WALK AWAY: Take pleasure in watching the cheese begin to sweat, then bubble, then pop and turn a deep golden to dark brown. The key is to get those teardrops of blobby cheese to run down the sides of the crocks and crisp up. Amazing! Serve hot.

If you prefer a lighter soup, use brown chicken stock instead of beef stock. At Caseus, we make chicken stock, beef stock, and veal stock, and when we have enough lamb scraps, we make rich, savory lamb stock. All have been used in our French Onion Soup.

Crab & Grapefruit over Zucchini Ribbons
w. Sheep's Milk Feta, 50

Buttercrunch Bacon & Blue, 54

Beet & Blue, 58

Arugula & Coppa w. Grilled Nectarine & Burrata, 60

Bacon, Egg & Cheese
w. Arugula, Deep-Fried Duck Egg & Gruyère, 62

Duck Confit Salad, 66

Salad Niçoise w. Chèvre Vinaigrette, 68

Caseus Caesar, 70

Grilled Halloumi w. Gulf Shrimp & Scallop Ceviche, 72

Heirloom Tomato & Fresh Pulled Mozzarella w. Saba
& Tuscan Olive Oil, 74

SALADS

OUR SALADS ARE BIG, MEANT TO BE EATEN AS A MEAL, and will satisfy. For me, a simple salad can be the foundation of a great dish. Local seasonal greens eaten when just harvested need only the simplest of dressings, the addition of a banging good cheese, and not always, but every so often, a bit of protein in the form of a fresh local egg or seared scallop. A salad's simplicity is the key to its success. If the ingredients are fresh, local, and vibrant, they only need be combined raw and uncomplicated, with the dressing serving as an equalizer to keep them connected with one another.

crab & grapefruit over zucchini ribbons
w. sheep's milk feta

Crab and grapefruit?! That's what I said when Chris, one of our young chefs, brought it up for us to taste one summer afternoon. But it just worked so right: the buttery crab playing off of the tart grapefruit, some zucchini ribbons holding it all up from underneath, our light Cured Lemon Dressing, the creaminess of good French sheep's milk feta, and just a few pieces of bitter frisée to bring you back to earth.

FEEDS: 4

2 large ruby grapefruit

1 pound lump crabmeat

1 medium zucchini

1 small head frisée

Cured Lemon Vinaigrette (page 144)

Prudent pinch of Maldon salt

Freshly ground black pepper

½ pound sheep's milk feta

This dish goes great with a cold bottle of Moscatel Seco, a Spanish muscat wine made dry but still loaded with flowering citric aromas and a silky mouth feel.

1. Supreme your grapefruit. What does that mean? It means to remove only the flesh of the citrus fruit without any pith or membrane. Lay the grapefruit on a cutting board and cut the top and bottom off so that some flesh is showing. Now, starting at the top and using a boning knife, cut off the skin as well as the pith, curving your knife to the contour of the fruit. Do this all around the fruit until you are left with just flesh showing, no pith or membrane at all. Hold the fruit in your left hand (right hand if you are left-handed) over a bowl, and, using a paring knife, cut along each section, removing the flesh only. When you are finished, you will have only the membrane left and all of the supremes will have been cut out. Squeeze as much of the juice from the membrane "star" as you can get into the bowl and reserve. Do this for both of the grapefruit. This step may seem hard, but it's not. Once you get good at this with a little practice, you'll never eat citrus any other way.

2. Remove the supremes from the bowl and add the lump crabmeat to the juice. Toss lightly and set aside.

3. With a vegetable peeler, make long ribbons of zucchini. You can take off a nice piece of finger doing this, so lay the zucchini down on a cutting board and go slowly. The saltiness of your blood will ruin the delicate flavors in this dish.

4. In a bowl, lightly dress the frisée and zucchini ribbons with a little Cured Lemon Vinaigrette, and season with some Maldon and fresh ground pepper.

5. To plate, arrange the zucchini ribbons on a chilled plate and top with the frisée. Then add the crabmeat and the grapefruit supremes, and crumble some feta on top. Finish it all off with a few hearty grinds of black pepper.

tommy& kelly

TITLE: Brother Man, Tommy, The Management

BIRTHPLACE: New Haven, Connecticut

HOBBIES: Cars, computers, web design, motorcycles, apple picking.

FAVORITE DISH TO MAKE AT HOME:
Hot cheese tortellini stirred together with fresh mozzarella, extra-virgin olive oil, cracked pepper, and some diced heirloom tomatoes stolen from Caseus for best flavor.

WHAT DO YOU LOVE ABOUT CASEUS?
Cheese. I like the staff . . . some of them . . . ha ha ha ha [laughing] . . . I like the customers too . . . some of them . . .

FAVORITE CASEUS MEAL? The BLT lobster roll is ridiculous. A couple rounds of the barbecue also rock. And the cheeseburger en croute we did a while back is memorable.

TITLE: Wife, Captain, Enforcer

BIRTHPLACE: New Haven, Connecticut

HOBBIES: School, walking and playing with my dog, *90210* reruns, reading, gardening, eating! College basketball!

FAVORITE DISH TO MAKE AT HOME:
Pastine and butter.

WHAT DO YOU LOVE ABOUT CASEUS?
Sometimes not a ton 'cause Jason is there ALL the time, but I do love the staff and a bunch of the regulars. I love the Bonde Montais goat cheese. It's one of my favorites.

FAVORITE CASEUS MEAL? Mac n Cheese with ham and peas and a good douse of Tabasco sauce.

buttercrunch bacon & blue

Ever go to a crappy diner at 3:00 A.M. and not know what to get? I find myself in this situation all too often. After many a bad decision (Salisbury steak, stuffed sole . . .), I've come to the conclusion that the BLT is always a surefire bet. This salad is based on the combination of savory crunchy bacon, crisp lettuce, bright tomato (if in season), and creamy buttermilk herb dressing.

FEEDS: 4

2–3 heads buttercrunch lettuce

If you can't find this, Bibb will do.

½ pound or more good slab bacon

If you must use something presliced, be sure it's thick-cut so you can make lardons.

1 cup finely chopped herbs

Tarragon, parsley, chervil, marjoram, basil, or dill—any combination of these works well.

½ cup buttermilk

3 tablespoons good red wine vinegar

¼ cup crème fraîche

We use Vermont Butter and Cheese Creamery (VBC), as it's the best I've found.

Kosher salt and freshly ground black pepper

1 large, juicy, seasonal heirloom tomato (optional)

½ pound Fourme d'Ambert blue cheese

Other blues will also work, but nothing too powerful, as you don't want to overrun the lettuce.

1. Start by gently breaking the heads of lettuce open. They're small and the leaves get smaller and crispier as you work your way to the center. Separate the leaves, doing your best to keep them whole. They may need a light rinse to remove the dirt, depending on where you got them. If the lettuce is grown organically and looks clean on the inside, just a little spritz of water will do. Shake the heads gently and pat them as dry as possible.

2. Cut ½-inch cubes of bacon and put them in a heavy-bottomed sauté pan over medium heat. Good bacon will have more than enough fat to slowly crisp up to a dark, delicious brown. Breathe in that bacon aroma—there is nothing more satisfying than bacon bubbling away in its own fat. Once crispy, take the lardons out and drain on a brown paper bag or paper towel.

3. In a large bowl, gently whisk the herbs, buttermilk, vinegar, and crème fraîche to combine. You can add salt and pepper to taste and a splash of water to thin it out if you like. It should not be thick, but more of a vinaigrette consistency.

4. Very lightly dress the lettuce leaves and neatly stack them. If you're using tomato, slice it thickly, and dress and stack the slices in between the lettuce or beside it—however you like.

5. Top the salad with the lardons and some blue cheese cut or crumbled to perfection. Like most salads, a healthy dose of fresh cracked pepper is essential on this one just before serving.

Wash it down with a bottle of cheap Italian Lambrusco, dry and slightly effervescent. A crusty baguette brings it all to perfection.

We get our buttercrunch lettuce from local farmer Brenda at Friends of Boulder Knoll, which is based two towns over in Cheshire. Brenda's small farm has a hard time keeping up with our demand, so this salad is usually only made once or twice a week. The little heads are super buttery, light, and crunchy—hence the name.

brenda

TITLE: Farmer

BIRTHPLACE: New Haven, Connecticut

HOBBIES: I practice the Japanese martial art of aikido. I also enjoy working on environmental and community projects; caring for our alpacas, cats, chickens, and ducks (including our female Rouen duck, Cheese); hiking; kayaking; and doing and seeing anything in Maine. I'm learning to spin and crochet with our alpacas' fleece. And, come to think of it, my work as a grower is my hobby too—there's so much to learn! I'm still amazed that huge plants grow from tiny seeds.

FAVORITE DISH TO MAKE AT HOME: A bowl of raspberries off of our own bushes, a Fudgsicle after a hot day, a stew made from veggies that we grew, and some good, grass-fed beef, lamb, or buffalo.

WHAT DO YOU LOVE ABOUT CASEUS? I love the passion that all of the staff has for preparing and serving locally sourced, fresh food. And I love all of their great tattoos—and the smell of cheese!

FAVORITE CASEUS MEAL? Anything Joe puts in front of me! How about the wild boar stew?! Not to mention the risotto with the poached duck egg; the seared scallops with heirloom tomatoes; the barbeque; braised greens; the mac and cheese; the *pommes frites;* and so on.

FRESH greens.

beet & blue

Not only are they sweet in flavor, loaded with energy-enhancing vitamin B, and absolutely beautiful to look at, beets are also a great local vegetable that we are able to get nearly year-round from our area sources. We always have them on our menu, and their color and taste suit both the harsh New England winters and those sticky summers. This recipe is a great wintertime version that uses a local cow's milk blue cheese from Cato Corner Farm in Colchester, Connecticut. In the summer we substitute a local goat's milk cheese from Lebanon, Connecticut for a lighter salad.

FEEDS: 4

4 large beets (softball size)

3 tablespoons peanut oil (or canola, if you're allergic to peanuts)

Kosher salt and freshly ground black pepper

This salad is beautiful and absolutely satisfying, much like my wife, Kelly.

FOR THE BEETS:

1. Preheat oven to 400°F.

2. Wash the beets under cold water and pat dry. Toss with the peanut oil and a bit of kosher salt and pepper. Place them on a baking sheet and bake the beets for about 1 hour, checking with the tip of a paring knife for doneness. (Different-size beets will take more or less time, so you'll need to stay on top of them.) If the knife inserts into the beets easily and comes out quickly, the beets are done. If not, allow to cook longer.

3. Once cooked, remove the beets from the oven and, while still hot, use a kitchen towel designated for this purpose (it will be purple after this procedure—you've been warned) to rub each beet until its skin is removed. Allow the beets to cool and then rinse them under cold water.

4. Cut the beets into slices or matchsticks (your preference).

Juice of 2 lemons

4 tablespoons extra-virgin olive oil

Kosher salt and freshly ground black pepper

FOR THE DRESSING:

Whisk the lemon juice and olive oil vigorously until emulsified. This step can be done in a blender, but the dressing should look rustic and slightly separated. Season with kosher salt and freshly ground black pepper to taste.

Several handfuls of light greens, such as mâche, watercress, arugula, tatsoi, or miszuna

Candied walnuts (page 66)

6–8 ounces Cato Corner Blue, depending on your liking

Maldon salt

TO FINISH:

Lightly toss the salad greens with the dressing and plate. Place the beets on top of the greens and the walnuts on top of the beets. Finish with a light drizzle of dressing over the beets, some crumbled pieces of Cato Corner Blue, and a pinch of Maldon sea salt.

Walnuts are what we use, but if you don't have any on hand, pecans, hazelnuts, almonds, or even peanuts are all great to add some crunch and sweetness.

arugula & coppa w. grilled nectarine & burrata

Juicy, curdy, peppery, fatty, and spicy—what else could you ask for on a summer night? This salad is so easy, it could be made by a blind dog with three legs and good taste.

FEEDS: 4

2 ripe nectarines

4 handfuls baby arugula

Great extra-virgin olive oil

Maldon salt and freshly ground black pepper

2 whole fresh burrata

Local honey

¼ pound coppa

Good balsamic vinegar

1. Preheat a charcoal grill (preferable) or a propane grill so that it's cranking hot.

2. Cut the nectarines in half and take out the pits. Put them aside for later.

3. Put the arugula in a large bowl and lightly dress with a drizzle of olive oil, salt, and freshly ground pepper.

4. Divide the dressed arugula onto 4 plates.

5. Cut the burrata in half and place one half on each plate with the cut side up.

6. Grill the nectarines cut side down for about 2–5 minutes. Be sure to get a nice caramelization, but don't burn them.

7. Place the grilled nectarine halves next to the burrata so their heat begins to soften the cheese. Drizzle the nectarines with a bit of local honey and more black pepper.

8. Complete the salad by adding a few thin slices of coppa to the plate.

9. Drizzle the burrata with olive oil and a touch of balsamic, and season with Maldon salt and fresh cracked pepper.

BURRATA VS. FRESH MOZZARELLA

Burrata is a form of fresh mozzarella that has added cream. A piece of newly formed fresh mozzarella is stuffed with the fresh mozzarella curd and fresh cream. It produces a ball of cheese with a soft liquid curdy inside. Fresh mozzarella has the same consistency throughout while burrata will almost explode when cut into.

Good subsititutions for burrata are mozzarella di bufala (real Italia buffalo mozzarella) or just plain mozzarella that is extremely fresh. But truly there is no real substitution for a great piece of burrata.

bacon, egg & cheese w. arugula, deep-fried duck egg & gruyère

Yes, another salad with bacon . . . getting the point yet? We make our own bacon here. Starting with fresh Berkshire bellies from Iowa, we cure 'em with kosher salt, local maple syrup, and tellicherry pepper. Then we slow smoke 'em over apple and peach wood. It's the pinnacle of baconness! Because our piggy bellies get to live outside even in the winter, they develop the true fat a pig is meant to have. When rendered off, this fat is plentiful in quantity and flavor. Reserve it for cooking anything from pancakes to eggs to fish. Bacon fat is where it's at.

FEEDS: 4

½ small red onion, thinly sliced

½ cup cider vinegar

½ pound good slab bacon

If you must use something presliced, be sure it's thick-cut so you can make decent lardons.

1 quart or so peanut oil (canola oil, if you're allergic)

½ cup sherry vinegar

Pedro Ximenez is best, but any nice one works.

Kosher salt and freshly ground black pepper

4 large handfuls wild arugula

Look for the spiciest variety you can find.

½ pound Gruyère

Rolf Beeler or Alpage is preferred, but if you're on a budget, cave-aged is also fine.

4 fresh duck eggs

Look for them at your local farmers' market or Asian grocery store.

1. Place the onions in the cider vinegar and allow to pickle gently. This can be done as far ahead as 24 hours.

2. Cut your bacon into nice-size lardons, about ¼-inch cubes. In a heavy sauté pan over medium heat, render them slowly until brown and crisp. Set aside; reserve some of the hot bacon fat.

3. Heat the oil to 375°F in a small saucepan (or fryer if you have one). The oil should be about 2 inches up the pan.

4. Meanwhile, combine 1 tablespoon of the warm bacon drippings with the sherry vinegar and whisk until emulsified. Season the dressing with salt and pepper to taste.

5. Lightly dress the arugula with the sherry bacon fat vinaigrette and divide evenly into 4 large, deep, chilled soup bowls. Top each salad with some pickled red onion and a few long, vegetable peeler ribbons of Gruyère.

6. Crack one of the duck eggs into a small mug or glass, then drop it into the preheated peanut oil. After about 40–60 seconds, or when the egg looks nicely browned and holds together, remove it with a slotted spoon onto a brown paper bag to drain. Repeat with the three other eggs and then top each salad with a deep-fried duck egg.

7. Finish the salads with copious amounts of crispy lardons and a heavy grind of fresh black pepper. The yolks of the deep-fried duck eggs should be runny and creamy while the whites should create whips that crunch and pop.

There is nothing more satisfying than breaking open a perfectly runny egg. Practice this—its importance is paramount.

duck confit salad

Needing a reason to put duck confit on something else, we put this simple salad together, and it has been a hit ever since. My wife, Kelly, orders it without the duck. I love her very much, but, Kel, what's the point?

FEEDS: 4

1 cup kosher salt

½ cup peppercorns

4 sprigs fresh thyme

1 sprig rosemary

5 cloves garlic

4 large duck legs

1 quart or more rendered duck fat

FOR THE DUCK CONFIT:

1. A day or preferably two before you want to have your duck confit, mix the salt, peppercorns, thyme, rosemary, and garlic together and rub all over the duck legs. Put the legs in a lidded container and place in the refrigerator for up to 12 hours; overnight is best.

2. When ready to cook, preheat oven to 300°F.

3. Take out the duck legs and wipe them clean of the salt, but not too thoroughly. Remove excess moisture by patting them with a towel. Place the legs in a large Dutch oven and cover them as completely as possible with the rendered duck fat.

4. On the stove, heat the legs and fat until the fat is clear and purely liquid, then put the uncovered pot in the preheated oven. Let cook for at least 4 hours or until the duck legs are super tender. Remove the legs from the fat and allow to cool completely.

2 cups shelled and lightly toasted walnuts

1 teaspoon kosher salt

1 teaspoon freshly ground black pepper

1 teaspoon brown sugar

1 teaspoon ground cayenne pepper

2 teaspoons orange juice

2 teaspoons unsalted butter, melted

FOR THE CANDIED WALNUTS:

1. Preheat oven to 300°F.

2. Toss the walnuts and the rest of the ingredients in a bowl until the nuts are evenly coated. Spread them out onto a parchment-lined baking sheet and put in the oven for 5–7 minutes. Take them out and move them around with a spatula, then put them back in the oven until lightly browned, about another 5–7 minutes. This can be done a few days ahead, and the nuts can be held in a lidded plastic container.

A mellow, not too overbearing French cabernet works as a complement here, but for this dish I like a Cab France with lots of earthiness and acidic red fruit flavors in the background. Or go the opposite way, if the weather permits, and get a huge, black cherry bomb Zinfandel from California; it works wonders with the fatty, crisp duck confit.

1. Supreme the oranges; that is, remove only the flesh of the fruit without any pith or membrane. Lay an orange on a cutting board and cut the top and bottom off so that some flesh is showing. Starting at the top, use a boning knife to cut off the skin as well as the pith, curving your knife to the contour of the fruit. Do this all around the fruit until you are left with just flesh showing, no pith or membrane at all. Hold the fruit in your left hand (right hand if you are left-handed) over a bowl, and, using a paring knife, cut along each section, removing the flesh only. When you are finished, you will have only the membrane left and all of the supremes will have been cut out. Squeeze as much of the juice from the membrane "star" as you can get into the bowl and reserve with the supremes. Do this for both of the oranges.

2. Set aside the supremes and just combine the fresh orange juice with the cabernet vinegar and slowly drizzle in the olive oil. I like a lightly broken dressing, but if you want it emulsified, beat it vigorously with a whisk. Season with salt and pepper to taste.

TO COMPLETE THE SALAD:

1. In a medium heavy-bottomed saucepan, heat the peanut oil to about 375°F.

2. Put out 4 chilled, deep bowls.

3. In a small bowl, pour a few tablespoons of the orange cabernet vinaigrette over the shallots.

4. Dress the arugula with the orange cabernet vinaigrette.

5. Crack the candied walnuts using the underside of a pan over a cutting board, and add to the dressed arugula.

6. Divide the dressed arugula and walnuts and orange supremes into the 4 bowls and top with the shallots.

7. Place the confit duck legs in the preheated peanut oil and fry until the skin is crisp and lightly GBD—golden brown and delicious.

8. Place a crispy, hot confit duck leg atop each bowl of salad, top with Maldon and fresh cracked pepper, and serve immediately.

---

2 navel oranges

If you can find them, Cara Cara oranges are a ton of fun, with lots of sweet juice and a bright pink flesh.

¼ cup cabernet vinegar

We use Forvum cabernet vinegar.

¼ cup extra-virgin olive oil

Maldon salt and freshly ground black pepper

---

1 quart peanut oil

1 cup orange cabernet vinaigrette

2 shallots, sliced extremely thin

4 handfuls wild arugula

1 cup candied walnuts

Orange supremes

4 legs duck confit

Maldon salt and freshly ground black pepper

salad niçoise w. chèvre vinaigrette

Classic and classy, salad niçoise is as fun to say as it is to make and eat. To switch it up, you don't have to follow this recipe to a T. Use what you have, but build your niçoise around the idea of a perfect composition. Color, texture, and temperature contrasts all balance to form the perfect niçoise salad. This can be a hearty main dish or even served as an antipasta to a large group for simple picking.

FEEDS: 4

Kosher salt

12 ounces fresh, clean, bright ahi tuna

½ cup Cured Lemon Vinaigrette (page 144)

2 ounces fresh chèvre (left out to soften)

We like the Beltane Farm Herbes de Provence log for this recipe, but your favorite fresh chèvre will work.

12 small baby Yukon Gold potatoes

Or any waxy potato variety you have on hand; Red Bliss works great as well.

A good bunch of string beans, tips removed

Haricots verts if you can find them, but local fresh is more important.

2 heads fresh romaine lettuce

A few tablespoons of extra-virgin olive oil

Maldon salt and freshly ground black pepper

1 cup unpastuerized niçoise olives

2 soft-boiled eggs

8 *fillets boquerones* (Spanish white anchovies)

1. Bring a large pot of kosher salted water to a boil.

2. Meanwhile, divide your tuna into four 3-ounce portions. Set aside to be grilled or pan-seared later, just before serving.

3. Place the Cured Lemon dressing and softened chèvre in a small bowl and beat with a whisk until combined. The dressing should look creamy but not be thick. If need be, thin with additional Cured Lemon Vinaigrette.

4. Once your salted water is at a hard, rapid boil, drop the potatoes in the water and boil until tender, about 10 minutes. Remove and set aside to dry and come to room temperature.

5. Drop the green beans into the boiling salted water for 40 seconds, then transfer them quickly into a bowl of ice water. They should be deep green but still very firm and crisp.

6. Split the heads of romaine in half lengthwise, and drizzle with extra-virgin olive oil, kosher salt, and freshly ground pepper.

7. Preheat a gas grill or get some coals going. You can also use a grill pan if you have one. Grill the romaine halves cut side down until lightly marked and caramelized, about 1 minute.

8. With the grill super hot, salt and pepper the tuna and drizzle with a little olive oil. Sear on the grill until the outside has a nice grill mark on all sides but the fish is still very rare; less than a minute on each side.

9. Construct your salads on 4 plates. Each gets a grilled romaine half, 3 boiled potatoes, a small pile of green beans, a little mound of olives, a half of a soft-boiled egg, a piece of seared tuna cut into neat even slices, and 2 fillets of boquerones. Spoon the chèvre vinaigrette over all of the ingredients, and finish with lots of fresh pepper and a sprinkle of Maldon sea salt.

SOFT BOILED EGG TIPS

Use older eggs; they're easier to peel. Prick each egg with a needle to allow steam to help with peeling. Use eggs that are stored at room temperature. Bring a pot that is small enough to just cover the eggs you're cooking within an inch of water. Bring the water to a boil then submerge the eggs into the pot and set a timer for 6 minutes. The yolks will be ever so slightly runny, but not super runny. Perfect for this salad.

caseus caesar

Et tu Brute? Yes, us too—we do a Caesar salad. It's traditional—we like tradition. It's straightforward—we like that too. Do we change it up to make it our own? Of course we do! Romaine is discarded for escarole, a more toothsome green not often eaten raw but, when dressed properly, holds up nicely against creamy dressing without getting soggy. And it stands on its own with crunchy croutons and salty pickled Spanish white anchovies (*boquerones*).

FEEDS: 4

1 large head escarole

4 slices pancetta (we use La Quercia)

½ crusty baguette

½ cup Cured Lemon Vinaigrette (page 144)

2 tablespoons house mayonnaise (page 143)

2 tablespoons champagne vinegar

10 *fillets boquerones*

5 sprigs fresh thyme, plus more for garnish

1½ cups finely grated Bianco Sardo

Any pecorino you like will do, but try not to use the mass-produced Pecorino Romano.

½ small red onion, thinly sliced

A hunk of Parmigiano Reggiano

Freshly ground black pepper

1 lemon, cut into quarters

Want to get really crazy? Try it with Tuscan kale too!

1. Pull the tougher first layer of outer leaves off the escarole and discard. Cut the butt end of the escarole off and discard. Cut the escarole with a sharp knife into 1-inch ribbons. Let sit in a sink or large bowl filled with cold water for a few minutes to clean. Rinse thoroughly and pat dry or spin dry.

2. While the escarole is drying, cut the pancetta slices into a small dice. In a medium pan, render the pancetta slowly so that it gets nicely crisp. This will take some time and attention to turn it every once in a while. When the pancetta bits are crispy, remove from the pan, saving any rendered fat. Let the bits cool on a brown paper bag or towel off to the side.

3. To make croutons, cut the baguette in half lengthwise and pull out all of the insides, making two boats of bread. (You can use the doughy white insides of the baguette for bread crumbs. They are not needed for this recipe anymore.) Cut the bread boats into ½-inch strips of U-shaped crust.

4. Heat the pan with the pancetta renderings over low to medium heat and add the bread. Toss to coat lightly. Not enough to coat? Add some olive oil. Season the croutons and toast in the pan until nicely browned and crispy. If you need to, throw them in the oven at about 350°F for 10 minutes. Reserve for later.

5. For the dressing, combine in a blender the Cured Lemon Vinaigrette, homemade mayo, vinegar, 2 of the fillets of boquerones, and the thyme stripped from its stems, as well as 2 tablespoons of the grated pecorino. If necessary, throw a few splashes of water in the blender to get the consistency of a nice, thin vinaigrette. Now blend, baby, blend!

6. In a large bowl, toss the escarole with your desired amount of dressing. Caesar salad should be dressed just right—not too much to make things heavy, but certainly enough to coat each leaf of escarole completely with a thin layer. Toss in the rest of the grated pecorino to coat the dressed escarole.

Spring has Sprung
CHEESES FOR THE SEASON:
Pave Sauvage
Midnight Moon
Bonne Bouche
Humbolt Fog
Crottin Fraise
Fleur de Maquis
Twig Farm

7. To plate, divide the dressed, cheese-laced escarole onto 4 chilled plates. Top each with crispy pancetta bits, toasted croutons, some onion slices, a few boquerones, and some vegetable peeler ribbons of the Parmigiano Reggiano. Garnish each salad with some fresh thyme pulled from the stem, copious amounts of coarsely ground black pepper, and a lemon wedge.

grilled halloumi w. gulf shrimp & scallop ceviche

Two worlds collide when you take a Greek grilling cheese and combine it with the inherently Peruvian technique of ceviche. The idea of cooking a cheese on a grill with no bread and no pan is at first a bit unfathomable. Likewise, eating shrimp and scallops cooked in acid will warrant the same response from some. This dish combines these two techniques for a powerhouse of flavor and texture, along with the dual feelings of refreshment and comfort, all rolled into one hell of an easy summer meal.

FEEDS: 4

1 pound day-boat scallops

1 pound Gulf shrimp, peeled and cleaned

Juice of 3 lemons

Juice of 5 limes

1 tablespoon champagne vinegar

3 serrano chilies, finely diced

¼ cup finely diced red onions

1 clove fresh garlic, thinly sliced

1 ripe heirloom tomato, diced small

Kosher salt and freshly cracked black pepper

2 packs Halloumi

Good Tuscan extra-virgin olive oil for lots of drizzlin'

4 large slices crusty baguette

4 fresh scallions

½ cup finely chopped cilantro

If you do not like cilantro, you're strange. But I understand some don't like it, so if you don't, substitute flat-leaf parsley.

1. About 2–3 hours before serving, clean and de-foot the scallops. Slice them in half so you have two disks per scallop. Cut the shrimp in half lengthwise. Try to make the shrimp and scallops similar in size; this way, the citrus will cook them evenly.

2. In a deep bowl, combine the lemon and lime juice, vinegar, serrano chilies, red onions, garlic, and tomato. Taste this and add kosher salt and fresh ground pepper to taste. Add the scallops and shrimp. Cover and refrigerate for 2–3 hours or until the shrimp and scallops become opaque and firmer to the touch.

3. Each pack of Halloumi contains two slabs of cheese. Carefully separate the slabs so they are even in size. Drizzle with a bit of olive oil and set aside to come to room temperature.

4. Heat a grill pan, gas grill, or charcoal grill to high. Grill each of the four slabs of Halloumi directly on the grill, allowing them to form a crisp, dark brown crust. Only flip them once. Meanwhile, grill the thick slabs of bread and the scallions with some of the olive oil, kosher salt, and fresh ground pepper.

5. To serve, divide the finished ceviche into 4 chilled bowls. If you've got boards (see cheeseboards, page 4), use them here. Plate a piece of grilled bread with a slab of grilled Halloumi, drizzle with olive oil, and grind lots of fresh cracked pepper on top. Do not add salt, as Halloumi is plenty salty. On the other end of each board, put a bowl of ceviche. Finish each bowl with fresh chopped cilantro and a healthy drizzle of olive oil. This dish works perfectly with a big bottle of chilled Grüner Veltliner, a guzzleable Austrian wine with tons of citrus and green grass flavors.

heirloom tomato & fresh pulled mozzarella
w. saba & tuscan olive oil

Feeling brave? This dish is best made by the stout of mind and thick of skin! Nothing, and I mean nothing, is better than freshly pulled mozzarella. When still warm, it travels like molten lava, stretching and reacting against the bright acidity of seasonal heirloom tomatoes. I'd venture to say that not too many people have experienced this cheese moments after it's been pulled. Want to impress a girl, wow your friends, and burn a few layers of skin off your hands? This recipe is for you!

FEEDS: 4

2 pounds fresh mozzarella curd

Several fresh, ripe heirloom tomatoes

1 bunch fresh basil

Grow some of your own basil; it's really easy and the best flavor you can get when picked as needed.

Saba for drizzlin'

This is a basic cooked-down vinegar—thick, intense, and sweet.

Tuscan extra-virgin olive oil for drizzlin'

Maldon salt and freshly ground black pepper

Prosecco works nicely with this dish, as does a heavily chilled cava. But for me, a glass of red sangria tops them all.

1. Bring a large pot of water to a rapid boil and salt it heavily. Give it a taste. Taste like seawater? You're all set then. Place a bowl of ice water as well as an empty bowl on the counter. Take the salted water off the stove and let it rest to slightly cool off.

2. Divide the "moot-z" curd into 4 equal pieces. One at a time, break the pieces of fresh curd into smaller pieces, about ½ inch in size. With a large ladle, put some of the rested, boiled salt water in the bowl with the curd. Let sit for about 20 seconds.

3. Now the fun begins. Plunge your hands into the bowl of ice water and get them nice and cold. Now plunge them into the hot water with the curd and scoop as much of it together as you can without really hurting yourself—embrace the pain, this is training for the rapture.

4. Push all of the softened mozzarella together to form a crude ball. Flatten and pull the ball gently. Now fold the curd into itself and pinch the ends, making a nice ball. Set aside. Repeat for the three other balls.

5. Place the fresh balls into warmed, deep bowls. Top with chunks of tomato, tears of basil, a drizzle of saba and the best olive oil you have, and a little Maldon salt and fresh cracked pepper. This must be consumed immediately. The soft, fresh cheese will ooze if kept nicely warm, filling the bottom of the bowl.

With this dish the cheese and tomatoes with the vinegary sweet saba and velvety olive oil take center stage.

Steak Frites, 80 * Moules Frites, 82

The Mac n Cheese, 85 * The Caseus Grilled Cheese, 86

The Cheeseburger, 90 * Roast Chicken, 92

Marcona Almond Pesto Pasta, 95

Braised Butt w. Collards & Jalapeño Chèvre Hushpuppies, 96

Lamb Kabobs over Cured Lemon Quinoa w.
Old Chatham Sheep's Milk Yogurt Tzatziki, 100

Peach & Chèvre Ravioli w. Thai Basil Brown Butter, 102

Lavender-Rubbed Lamb Leg Steak w. Dandelion Mashed Potatoes
& Sheep's Milk Feta Gremolata, 106

Ricotta Gnocchi w. Butternut Squash, Fried Sage & Sbrinz, 108

Blackened Catfish w. Avocado Jicama Salad
& Chipotle Chèvre Quesadillas, 110

Caseus Wellington, 112

BIG PLATES

Here are the meat and potatoes. Our first-ever dish, Steak Frites, is as classic and straightforward as it gets. At Caseus, big plates mean *big* plates. At its heart, Caseus is a gastropub. Come in here hungry, and we'll be sure to satiate your desires with tweaked classics—big, hearty, and warming. Growing up in an adventurous quasi-vegetarian household, I was exposed to all sorts of main course abominations: meatless meat loaf made with Special K and soy gravy, "TLT" sandwiches consisting of cardboard-textured whole-grain bread, lettuce, tomatoes, and skillet-browned tofu. For my restaurant, a big plate means a 12-ounce pasture-raised, grass-fed skirt steak with globs of sage unsalted butter melting on top and a gargantuan pile of fries laced with kosher salt and ground pepper, with a nice ramekin of house-made fresh mayonnaise riding shotgun on the plate. If this doesn't make your cheeks pinch in anticipation, go back to the salad section, whip up something nice and light, and enjoy your Lifetime movie.

steak frites

My first Steak Frites experience was at a little bistro in Montreal called Le Express. I was told I had to try this particular dish there. Steak and fries, I thought. What's the big deal? When done correctly, it is a very big deal. Nothing could be more straightforward and basic and yet so utterly satisfying! Add a fresh-made mayo to dip your savory steak and crisp, salty fries into, and you've got one of the best darn dinners around. I recommend a salad to accompany this for color contrast, but it's really not necessary.

We use grass-fed skirt steak at Caseus, which gives us a wonderfully flavored piece of meat, still laden with fat and real beef flavor. I recommend using cuts like flank, skirt, and hanger for the Steak Frites, and if possible, grass-fed beef is always best. Not only does it taste better, but it's easier to digest and better for you and the environment.

FEEDS: 2

2 12-ounce skirt steaks, trimmed of fat

1 bunch fresh rosemary

6 cloves fresh garlic, peeled then smashed with the side of a knife

Good extra-virgin olive oil

Kosher salt and freshly ground black pepper

Frites (page 12)

House mayonnaise (page 143)

1. Marinate steaks with fresh rosemary, garlic, and olive oil overnight in the fridge.

2. Preheat grill on high (use hard charcoal, if possible).

3. Salt and pepper the steaks liberally (1 tablespoon of each spread all over each steak).

4. Throw the steaks on the preheated grill until cooked to a perfect medium-rare, 2 minutes per side of each steak. Remove from the grill.

5. Let the steaks rest for at least 5 minutes. Slicing against the grain, cut each steak into ¼-inch-thick slices. Fan slices onto a warmed plate. Serve with a large pile of fresh, screaming hot, salty frites and fresh mayo.

You can change up your steak toppings to match the seasons. Here's what we recommend:

FALL: St. Agur or Gorgonzola Dolce
WINTER: rich red wine veal stock (see recipe page 141)
SUMMER: fresh thyme, sweet cream, and compound butter

moules frites

There is no cheese in this dish, although due to its ridiculous quantity of butter and simple delicious preparation, it is and will always be synonymous with Caseus. It's a classic dish that we've not really messed around with too much. Doing the frites as an accompaniment is the best, but in a pinch for a Wednesday-night dinner with a large group of friends, a few grilled hunks of good bread rubbed with garlic are quite nice as well. Best tip is to get great PEI mussels and a really good white wine.

FEEDS: 2 FOR A MEAL, 8 AS AN APPETIZER

5 dozen Prince Edward Island mussels

½ pound fresh unsalted butter

4 cloves garlic, minced

2 large shallots, minced

3 slices cured lemons (page 138), minced

Good pinch of kosher salt

Few good grinds of fresh cracked black pepper

Pinch of dried crushed red pepper

3 cups good, crisp white wine, nothing oaky

Frites (page 12) or grilled rustic bread

Sur Lie Clos des Briords Muscadet is the perfect Loire white wine for Moules Frites. Briny and acidic at the same time, it balances with the sweet mussels like nothing else. Although a nice, cold Abbey Leffe or Houblon Chouffe ain't too bad either.

1. Clean the mussels by using a nail brush to scrub them really well in ice-cold running water. Pull any scraggles off of them. If any are broken or don't close up when tapped on the side of the sink, chuck 'em. Once they're all nicely cleaned, set them aside in a large bowl. If you're not going to use them immediately, put them in the fridge until you're ready.

2. Combine the butter, garlic, shallots, cured lemons, salt, ground black pepper, and crushed red pepper in a large stock pot or sauce pot, or two smaller sauce pots, over medium to high heat. Let cook until all of the butter is melted and the shallots and garlic begin to sizzle, just a few minutes.

3. Turn the heat up to high and add the mussels all at once. Add the white wine and cover the pot immediately so none of the steam escapes. After a few minutes, give the pot a good stir so that the mussels on top get to have some time on the bottom.

4. Once they've opened up, you know they are completely cooked. Do not continue to cook the mussels for too much longer, as they will get rubbery. Undercooked, and they will have a slimy, soft texture. They should be wide open and appear plump when cooked perfectly.

5. Taste the broth. Adjust seasoning with salt and pepper.

6. To serve, dump the mussels into a large communal bowl. Cover with foil or another large bowl. Take to the table and uncover. The aromatic steam is sweet and a huge part of the mussel experience. Serve with fries or grilled bread.

the mac n cheese

It's not your momma's mac and cheese, but it's damn good! The Mac n Cheese is not consistent at Caseus. Natural things, artisanal things—especially cheese—are inconsistent. Throughout the year as the seasons change, we change our Mac n Cheese, adding more chèvre or more Raclette as we see fit. Sometimes the nubs, ends, and bits are different; this means the Mac n Cheese is as well. At any given time you may find the perfect Mac n Cheese combination for you, and although you'll search the rest of your life for it again and again, it—like your first kiss in fifth grade on the playground swings—may never be as extraordinary. It's the journey, not the destination, that the true epicure relishes.

FEEDS: 6–10

1. Preheat oven to 275°F.

2. Bring water to a boil in a large pot and add a good handful of salt to the water. Boil orecchiette until slightly undercooked, just before the al dente stage. Drain. Toss cooked pasta in a bowl with olive oil and set aside.

3. Slice brioche thin and place on a cooking sheet. Toast in the oven for 20 minutes or until dry but not overly brown. Remove, let cool, and crumble into small pieces. This will yield more bread crumbs than you need, but making them from scratch makes all the difference.

4. Increase oven temperature to 400°F.

5. Melt butter in a small pan. Whisk in flour until completely incorporated (no lumps). This is called a roux.

6. Crumble chèvre into small pieces and grate all the other cheese.

7. In a small sauce pot, bring milk to a boil, stirring occasionally. Add the roux, whisking constantly, until mixture returns to a boil. The mixture will thicken. Turn off the heat. You now have a béchamel sauce.

8. Add three-quarters of the cheese, whisking until melted and incorporated. Add nutmeg and season with salt and pepper to taste.

9. Add sauce to the cooked pasta and toss to coat. Place in an ovenproof dish, top with remaining cheese, and bake for 25 minutes or until bubbling hot.

10. Top with bread crumbs and continue to bake for 3–5 minutes. Remove from oven when dish becomes very oozy, bubbly, and GBD—golden brown and delicious.

1 pound orecchiette pasta

1 tablespoon extra-virgin olive oil

1 small loaf brioche or other enriched bread

⅓ cup unsalted butter

⅓ cup flour

¼ pound chèvre

⅔ pound extra-sharp Vermont cheddar

⅔ pound 2-year-aged Gouda

⅔ pound 12-month-aged Comté

⅔ pound Raclette, French or Swiss will do

¼ pound provolone

Any bits, ends, or leftover nubs of cheese you have kicking around in your fridge

1 quart milk

1 teaspoon freshly grated nutmeg

Plenty of Kosher salt and freshly ground black pepper

the caseus grilled cheese

The seasonality of cheese combined with our preference for particular tastes calls for different flavors as the year rolls through. Summer basks in cool briny fetas, fall blows in robust cheddars, winter warrants spicy blues, and spring rejuvenates us with bright, acidic goat's milk cheeses. Flavors aside, texture is key to making a great grilled cheese sandwich. Since this dish has only a few basic components, it is important to be conscious of all variables when making grilled cheese.

FEEDS: 1

3 tablespoons fresh unsalted butter at room temperature

We use Cabot Vermont unsalted butter, but get whatever you can that is local and fresh.

2 thick slices brioche or seeded rye (about 1-inch thick)

We use Sono Bakery in South Norwalk, Connecticut, or Lupi Legna Rye, in New Haven, Connecticut

½ to ¾ pound (depending on how cheesy you want it) shredded cheese mix

Whole-grain mustard

Cornichon pickles, or any acidic pickle of your choice

1. Preheat oven to 400°F.

2. Spread about 1 tablespoon of room-temperature butter on one side of each piece of bread. Evenly divide the cheese and place on the unbuttered side of each piece of bread to form two open-face sandwiches. Place the remaining butter in a pan over medium heat on the stove until it begins to foam but not turn brown.

3. Place the two slices, butter side down, cheese side up, in the pan and brown them evenly.

4. When the slices are nicely browned, place the entire pan in the oven for about 10 minutes or until the cheese is bubbling and hot.

5. Remove the pan from the oven and, with a spatula, put the sandwich together. Serve with whole-grain mustard and pickles on the side. This sandwich goes well with tomato soup (page 30), for dipping.

Depending on the season and availability, we use Comté, Gruyère, Raclette, Provolone, 2-year-aged Gouda, Emmentaler, and then anything else we can find that is in season. These cheeses are the base to create a great texture, but the addition of something new and seasonal makes the sandwich unique and truly wonderful.

jeff

TITLE: Cheese Truck Cheese Master

BIRTHPLACE: Royal Oak, Michigan

HOBBIES: Bicycle racing/riding, hiking, and family time.

FAVORITE DISH TO MAKE AT HOME: Crazy, mixed-up burritos.

WHAT DO YOU LOVE ABOUT CASEUS? The atmosphere, the staff, and the customers. It is the funnest place to be.

FAVORITE CASEUS MEAL? The list is long but includes scallops, mussels, and barbecue.

CASEUS

TheCheeseTruck.com

the cheeseburger

I had my first Billy burger many summers ago on a camping trip in upstate New York during a white-water rafting expedition with some friends. A nod to the inventor of the recipe—Billy's dad—the Billy burger looked like a charred-to-death hockey puck of a hamburger so overdone it should have tasted dry and cardboard-like. Instead, I bit into a really juicy, damn good hamburger. The secret to making a burger juicy even if charred to death, I learned, is to add some grape jelly to the meat. The pectin in the jelly helps to congeal the fat in the burger meat and makes it less apt to run out. Because you use such a small ratio of jelly to beef, the grape taste is completely undetectable. Purists might complain—let 'em. My version of the Billy burger is seriously good, even if someone asks for it incinerated to the point of well done.

FEEDS: 5–6

2 pounds grass-fed ground beef

I like to use 80/20, with 20 percent of the meat fat. It's this high-fat mix that makes the burger shrink when you cook it, but yields very juicy, flavorful burgers.

2 tablespoons grape jelly

Don't use an artisanal grape jelly—the cheaper and trashier the better.

Kosher salt and coarsely ground black pepper

1 pound extra-sharp Vermont cheddar

Cabot works, but if you can get some Shelburne Farms or Grafton Village, that's nice too.

Brioche bun, or whatever bread you love

We get ours from Sono Bakery in South Norwalk, made especially for us. They're big, soft, and rich and get nicely toasty.

Ketchup, mayo, and pickles (optional)

1. Mix the ground beef and grape jelly gently with your hands. Do not mix in any salt at this time!

2. Form 5 or 6 patties with your hands. They should be about 1 inch thick and nicely round. Try not to overwork the meat, as this makes it tough. Place the patties on a plate and hit with a bunch of salt and pepper. Feel free to add more salt; remember, there is none in the meat so you have to make up for the lack of seasoning, some of which will fall off during cooking.

3. Cover your burgers and let them sit out to come slightly up to room temperature. This will help them cook a bit faster and more evenly.

4. You'll need a charcoal grill, a char-broiler, or a good, well-seasoned cast-iron pan. If using a cast-iron pan and cooking indoors, you'll also need to use your oven. The process that follows is what we do indoors at the bistro, but if you're outside at home on the grill, the process of cooking your burger will be as follows: Build a pile of coals for direct heat on one side of the grill, with the other side empty. You'll sear the burgers over the direct heat and then move them to the cooler side and cover the grill to finish cooking them on the inside.

5. Preheat oven to 400°F.

6. Preheat your pan over medium heat. If it is not very well seasoned, you can place a tiny bit of vegetable oil in the pan, but you shouldn't need it with all the fat in the beef.

7. Lay the burgers in the pan, a couple at a time. Don't worry about getting them all in the pan at once. Cook each burger, flipping only once in the pan after a nice, thick, dark crust has formed. Transfer them to

a sheet pan and, when they are all cooked, place them in the preheated oven. The patties you cooked first will be medium to medium-rare while the ones you cooked last will be rare, depending on how long you cook them in the oven, which should be just a few minutes, depending on your desired temperature of doneness. You'll need to give them a little poke: soft is rare, hard is well done, and in between is medium-rare.

8. With a minute or so left before you take them out of the oven, hit the burgers with thick slices of cheese and throw your buns, sliced in half, in the oven.

9. Pull the burgers out and allow them to rest in the buns for a few minutes while you get the ketchup, mayo, and pickles ready. This allows the juices to move back to the center of the burger and cook slightly. Resting a burger is very important; most people overlook this step. Compile your burger, and enjoy.

Nothing goes better with a great burger than an ice-cold beer. For me, Belgium Palm is simply creamy and complements the beef wonderfully. It doesn't overwhelm, but has just enough flavor to quench your thirst from the salty, gamey, grass-fed beef.

roast chicken

We use a heritage breed of chicken called the Poulet Rouge at Caseus. It's not been genetically messed with in any way. They are chickens the way chickens have always been. The flavor speaks for itself—try to find organic and free-range chicken. Think heirloom tomatoes versus the industrially raised version. The other wonderful thing is that these chickens have no added hormones, genetic chemicals, or unwanted antibiotics. This is a huge plus, and it adds to the overall quality of the dish. The second secret is the brine. While adding flavor and seasoning it also helps the bird to cook evenly and keeps it super juicy and moist.

FEEDS: 2–3

3 quarts tap water

5 pounds ice

1 cup kosher salt

1 cup raw sugar

1 lemon, cut in half

Handful of black peppercorns

1 sprig fresh rosemary

1 sprig fresh thyme

1 2½–3 pound brined bird

1 large onion, sliced skin on into ¼-inch slices

2 cloves garlic, skin on

1 lemon

1 good nob (for me it's about 1 tablespoon) room-temperature unsalted butter

Kosher salt and freshly ground black pepper

1 bunch fresh thyme

FOR THE CHICKEN BRINE:

In a small saucepan, bring the 3 quarts of the water and the remaining ingredients to a boil. Pour the hot contents of the pan and the remaining 3 quarts of water into a large bowl or deep container and then add the ice. Check to be sure the mixture is very cold.

FOR THE ROAST CHICKEN:

1. Once the brine is completely cooled, submerge the chicken into the brine and refrigerate overnight or up to 8 hours. Don't let the chicken soak too much longer, as the meat will get mushy and not be very pleasant.

2. Preheat oven to 425°F. Later on when you put the bird into the oven, you'll reduce the temp. This little trick ensures a nice, crispy skin and relieves the oven from reheating after losing its preheat from your opening the oven door.

3. Remove the chicken from the brine and dry as thoroughly as possible with a paper towel. Do this over the sink to contain liquids. Let the bird sit on a plate in the fridge to dry slightly while you prepare the pan.

4. Cover the center of a large cast-iron skillet or roasting pan with the sliced onions. Throw in the garlic cloves and squeeze the lemon's juice all over the pan and onions.

5. Take the bird out of the fridge, and rub it down inside and out with the butter. Really get it in there.

6. Liberally salt and pepper the bird, both inside and out. Add half of the squeezed lemon to the cavity along with some of the fresh thyme.

7. Put the bird atop the onions, breast facing up, and tuck its legs and drumstick in. Gingerly toss the remaining thyme about the pan.

8. Pop the bird into the oven and lower the heat to 400°F. Allow to cook for about an hour or until the skin is crisp and blistered. Poke the thigh; if the juices run clear, it's more than done.

9. Remove the bird from the oven and allow it to rest for about 10–15 minutes.

Roast chicken should always be accompanied by a crisp white wine, like a Vino Verde or a Pinot Gris. Leftover, it's the perfect cold, quick breakfast to go—just grab a drumstick and thigh, and hop in the car to work.

You can make chicken gravy out of the pan juices, onions, garlic, and thyme. In the pan atop the stove, reduce a cup or two of white wine, apple cider, or even just water—all work great, but it depends on what you like. The addition of a blob of butter at the end is really nice to thicken the gravy just a bit.

marcona almond pesto pasta

When we opened Caseus, this dish was a staple on the menu. Since then, other dishes have taken its place. Lately, though, I've been getting tons of requests for the dish, so I thought it'd be fun to have it in our cookbook. After you've made this once, it is easy to do over and over again. Like our Mac n Cheese recipe, we use orecchiette for this one, which works nice to scoop up all the rich sauce. This is not your momma's light pesto. It's got cream, butter, and Marcona almonds, and it's freaking delicious!

FEEDS: 4–6

1. Bring a large pot of salted water to boil. Drop the basil into the boiling water for 2 seconds, then remove with a slotted spoon and place directly into a bowl of ice water to shock bright green. Drain and set aside to dry as completely as possible. This is a pain but will yield bright green pesto that won't turn brown on you.

2. In a food processor, add the olive oil, garlic, Pecorino Toscano, half the Parmigiano, and the blanched basil. Process until nicely combined. If need be, add more olive oil as you go to loosen the mixture. Add the Marcona almonds last and pulse lightly so they have some texture. Add salt and pepper to taste.

3. In the same pot of boiling water you used previously, cook your orecchiette until al dente, about 7–8 minutes.

4. While the pasta cooks, melt the butter in a large sauté pan. Add the pesto from the food processor and the cream to the pan with the melting butter. Stir it gently with a wooden spoon to combine. Add the orecchiette straight from the boiling water, using a slotted spoon or spider, and toss to coat completely.

5. Divide into 4–6 bowls (depending on how many you want to feed) and finish with the reserved Parmigiano and crushed Marcona almonds. You can garnish with a few fresh basil leaves if you're feeling really fancy. This dish is rich and creamy and insanely good. The sauce will look a bit soupy but will soak up into the ears as you stir it up.

¼ pound (or several bunches) picked basil

1 cup extra-virgin olive oil

2 cloves garlic, peeled

¼ cup grated Pecorino Toscano

½ cup grated Parmigiano Reggiano

¼ cup Marcona almonds, plus a few crushed for garnish

Kosher salt and freshly ground black pepper

1 pound (or so) orecchiette pasta

2 tablespoons fresh unsalted butter

1 cup cream

braised butt w. collards & jalapeño chèvre hushpuppies

The braised butt caused a nice little stir in the restaurant when it first hit the menu because of its name. When we took it off for the change of the season, the stir was that people didn't want to see it go. Basically a big ol' hunk of pork butt (also called the Boston butt or pork shoulder), the braised butt was just that—simple, braised, and wonderfully delicious. We took the fatty, tough piece of meat and cut it into a personal size, seasoned it, seared it, and braised it in local maple syrup and robust Kentucky bourbon. Accompanied by some chèvre jalapeño hushpuppies and simply braised collards, you've got a serious dinner that is perfect for the autumn season. This is by far one of my personal favorite dishes that we do, and fall is one of my most anticipated seasons because of it.

FEEDS: APPROXIMATELY 8

1 large pork butt (approximately 8–10 pounds)

Kosher salt and freshly ground black pepper (enough to coat the entire outside of the butt)

½ cup canola oil

2 cups real maple syrup

2 cups bourbon, plus 1 shot

We enjoy Jim Beam; it's not that expensive and is easily available.

2 cups tap water

1 large onion, peeled and cut into quarters

I like to cook the pork the night before I serve it and then reheat it the day of. The meat not only gets more tender as it sits overnight, but it also takes on more flavor.

FOR THE BRAISED BUTT:

1. Preheat oven to 185°F.

2. Cut the pork butt into several large cubes, about 4–5 inches by 4–5 inches square. They don't all have to be exact. Season each pork butt cube with a good amount of salt and pepper on all sides.

3. In a large pan, sear the outside of each cube in the canola oil until nicely brown. This step can be done in batches.

4. In a bowl, combine the maple syrup, 2 cups bourbon, and water. Pour the extra shot of bourbon into your mouth and swallow. Place the seared pork butt cubes snuggly together in a deep roasting pan and add the quartered onion. Pour the maple-bourbon-water mixture over the entire mess and cover tightly with foil.

5. Place into the preheated oven for 4–7 hours. You'll need to test the doneness of the pork as it cooks, as all butts are not alike. Cut into one of them with a knife after 4 hours to check for doneness. Sometimes they're ready by then, sometimes they aren't. You're looking for the knife to go in easily and be able to wiggle around. You don't want them to cook too long, or they'll get dry and fall apart too much. Reserve the braising liquid.

Pictured here with jalapeño-cheddar cornbread.

FOR THE COLLARDS:

1. Bring a large pot of salted water to boil. Drop the prepared greens into the boiling water and allow to cook for about 2 minutes. Transfer the greens into a bowl of ice water and stir to abruptly stop the cooking. Drain the greens as best you can, using a few kitchen towels to wick off any excess water.

2. In a large skillet over medium heat, melt the butter with the olive oil and add the garlic and shallots. Once nicely translucent, add the shocked greens and sauté until they are warmed through and slightly more tender. Add salt and pepper to taste. This recipe will yield a very toothsome collard green.

1 big bunch fresh collards, ribs removed, cut into 1-inch strips

2 tablespoons fresh unsalted butter

2 tablespoons olive oil

2 cloves garlic, finely chopped

3 large shallots, finely chopped

Kosher salt and freshly ground black pepper

This is not a traditional collard greens recipe. This is a refined and, in my opinion, easier and quicker way to cook greens. We use the blanching technique—the greens are boiled for a bit and then shocked to a bright green in ice water. They are then sautéed atop the stove with butter, olive oil, garlic, and shallots. Prepared this way, the greens are certainly toothier than those mushy Southern-style staples that I really love, but the vegetable taste shines through and works really well with the pork and hushpuppies.

keep going, next page >

1 quart peanut oil (for frying)

2 cups yellow cornmeal

3 tablespoons all-purpose (AP) flour

½ teaspoon baking soda

1 teaspoon baking powder

1 cup buttermilk, or 1 cup whole milk with 1 tablespoon cider vinegar

8 ounces fresh chèvre, allowed to sit out until soft

We use Beltane Farm from Lebanon, Connecticut.

1 egg

1 tablespoon kosher salt

2 jalapeños, ribs and stems removed, finely diced

FOR THE CHÈVRE JALAPEÑO HUSHPUPPIES:

1. Preheat peanut oil to 375°F in a heavy-bottomed deep pan or a deep fryer.

2. Mix all of the ingredients together until just combined and wet. Using an ice cream scoop, drop balls of the mixture into the preheated oil. Allow to cook in the oil until crisp and a deep golden brown, about 3 minutes, and then drain on brown paper bags or towels.

TO COMPLETE THE DISH:

1. In a saucepan, heat up all of the braising liquid that was in the roasting pan from the pork.

2. Place the pork into the saucepan and reheat one hunk per person.

3. While fried hushpuppies sit draining off excess oil, finish sautéing the collards.

4. To serve, give each plate a big ol' hunk of pork, then add some greens and a few hushpuppies. Lightly pour some of the slightly reduced braising liquid over the pork to make it glisten.

TITLE: Architect, Professor (would-be Gentleman Farmer)

BIRTHPLACE: District of Columbia, our nation's capital

HOBBIES: Rowing, habitat restoration, environmental advocacy, my garden and orchard, maple sugaring, chasing after my young boys.

FAVORITE DISH TO MAKE AT HOME: Gumbo. Once you have the basics covered, you can put almost anything into it, like available vegetables and herbs, leftovers, "cook-it-or-lose-it" meats, etc.

SPECIALTY IN THE KITCHEN: Letting nothing go to waste.

WHAT DO YOU LOVE ABOUT CASEUS? You mean besides the talented and attractive waitstaff? The honest, sincere, delicious, local food.

lamb kabobs over cured lemon quinoa w. old chatham sheep's milk yogurt tzatziki

A great summer or springtime dish, this is the easiest cut of lamb to cook. It cooks up quickly and always tastes phenomenal. Lamb loin—lean, clean, and still full-flavored—is also great because it can be cooked to a nice medium-rare and still be quite tender. We skewer a few chunks of the loin with red onions and sweet red peppers and grill them to order. This dish can be done without the skewers, of course, but meat is always fun to eat off of a stick. The vegetables give the meat a great flavor as they char and cook, their juices and scents adding to the entire experience. The lamb is seasoned with a specific Turkish spice blend that I learned from my former boss and Turk, Ihsan. With lamb, it just can't be beat.

FEEDS: 4

4 8-ounce lamb loins

4 tablespoons baharat

Kosher salt

2 red bell peppers, cut into 8 large chunks

2 smallish red onions, peeled and quartered

4 soaked wooden skewers, about 10 inches long

Said to be the Arabic word for spices, baharat can be found at most reputable spice shops and online.

4 cups quinoa

8 cups water

1 tablespoon salt

½ cup unsalted butter

4–6 slices cured lemons (page 138), sliced very small

Kosher salt and freshly ground black pepper

Fresh mint (optional)

FOR THE LAMB KABOBS:

1. Cut each of the lamb loins into 4 equal parts and season them with baharat and some kosher salt.

2. Evenly skewer the lamb, peppers, and onions onto the 4 skewers. Set aside to marinate for at least an hour while you prepare your grill. For best results, these kabobs should be cooked over hardwood coals. The intense heat and smoke really complete the dish and give the lamb a crusty outside with the spiced baharat.

3. Grill the kebobs until nice and crusty on all sides, about 1 minute or less per four sides. Let them rest while you plate up your quinoa.

We use all-natural lamb from Colorado. The taste is significantly different than the stuff from New Zealand and it is slightly pricier.

FOR THE QUINOA:

1. Rinse the quinoa at least 3 times in cold running water. The quinoa can get slimy if you don't do this.

2. Add the quinoa to a medium pot with the water and salt. Bring to a boil and let boil for 3 minutes. Turn off the heat and let sit, covered, for at least 15 minutes more. You do not want to cook it too long, as it will get mushy.

3. In a small saucepan, melt the butter until foaming and add the cured lemons. Fluff the cooked quinoa lightly with a fork, adding the butter and cured lemon mixture. Season to taste with salt and pepper and, if you have it, some fresh mint.

So what the hell is quinoa? It's a gluten-free ancient grain from South America high in amino acids and just plain darn delish! Unbelievably, it's in the same family as spinach and rainbow chard, and it's all the rage with the crunchy, healthy types. But don't let that sway you. Our recipe makes it taste damn good and adds what else but some butter to amp it up a bit.

FOR THE TZATZIKI:

1. Combine all of the ingredients, except the salt and pepper, in a food processor and pulse until nicely blended but still a bit chunky.

2. Season with salt and lots of freshly ground pepper to taste. Refrigerate for an hour before serving.

TO PLATE:

1. Divide the quinoa onto 4 plates and top with the nicely grilled kabobs.

2. Finish the entire plate with a nice spoonful of the tzatziki. For a delicious touch, add a few grilled lemon halves to squeeze onto the lamb and quinoa just before eating. Yum.

3 tablespoons extra-virgin olive oil

1 tablespoon red wine vinegar

2 cups Old Chatham Sheep's Milk Yogurt

3 cloves garlic, peeled

1 cucumber, peeled, cut in half, and seeds removed

Handful of fresh dill, torn up

Kosher salt and freshly ground black pepper

peach & chèvre ravioli w. thai basil brown butter

Peaches and basil were made for one another. Thai basil has a great anise quality to it that shines through all the other ingredients in this dish and really hits the spot. Peaches and chèvre are a theme for me. The Bucheron and grilled peach dessert is the origin of this dish (see page 133).

FEEDS: 4

2 cups semolina

2 cups flour

1 teaspoon salt

6 eggs

If sticking, add a few tablespoons of olive oil to the bowl before refrigerating overnight.

FOR THE RAVIOLI DOUGH:

1. In a kitchen mixer, mix the semolina, flour, and salt with the paddle attachment to combine.

2. Add the eggs one at a time with the mixer on low. Let the mixer knead the dough into a ball; if the mix looks really dry, add a couple table-spoons of cold water. Wrap the pasta dough up in plastic wrap and refrigerate overnight.

You'll have more pasta dough than you need for filling, but you can store the rest for use later. Make up some pasta sheets for another dinner.

For ease, you can use wonton wrappers for this dish in lieu of the pasta dough recipe. I won't judge you. At Caseus, we make a certain amount of raviolis each day when this dish is on the menu. When the raviolis run out, we're done serving the dish for the night.

FOR THE PEACH AND CHÈVRE FILLING:

1. With a paring knife, score the tops of the peaches with an X and drop them into a pot of boiling water. Boil for 1 minute and remove into a bowl of ice water. Peel away the fuzzy skin, then cut the peaches and remove the pits. Chop the peaches into a small dice. Reserve about ¼ cup of the diced peaches for later.

2. In a large bowl, mix the chèvre, ricotta, and beaten egg with the peaches, incorporating them nicely. Some of the peaches will smash up, but not all of them.

2 peaches

12 ounces fresh chèvre

Valençay is a great choice for this recipe.

¼ cup ricotta

1 egg, beaten

TO PREPARE THE RAVIOLIS:

1. Roll out the pasta dough into long sheets, and dollop a tablespoon of the filling onto the sheets, spaced apart by a few inches. Top each sheet with another thin sheet of rolled-out dough and, using a large glass, cut the ravioli out. Use your fingers dipped in water to press around each ravioli so they are tightly sealed.

2. Drop the ravioli a few at a time into a large pot of salted, boiling water and allow to boil gently until they rise to the top, no more than 2 minutes. If they break open, you need to seal them better.

3. In a large sauté pan, melt the butter slowly over medium to low heat until it foams and starts to turn light brown. Toss the ravioli into the pan and let them lightly brown with the butter. Tear the basil leaves and scatter them all about the pan. Then plate them up. No one will complain if you finish this dish off with a bit more cheese. More goat cheese or some simple grated Parmigiano is just perfection. Garnish with the reserved ¼-cup of diced peaches and pepper.

½ cup unsalted butter

Handful of Thai basil leaves, picked and cleaned

Handful of cheese of your choice (optional)

Lots of freshly ground black pepper

lavender-rubbed lamb leg steak w. dandelion mashed potatœs & sheep's milk feta gremolata

This is the ultimate springtime recipe. Lamb leg, usually a slow-roasted whole piece, is cut into slabs like a thick ham steak in cartoons, the circular bone just off-center in the middle. You can have your butcher do this for you and ask him to cut them about an inch or so thick. The dried lavender should be organic for this—no substitutions. The non-organic lavender is meant for eye pillows and not consumption, as they add pretty large amounts of pesticides. When the lavender burns, it perfumes the meat in a really glorious way.

FEEDS: 4

4 ounces sheep's milk feta

¼ cup good extra-virgin olive oil

½ cup coarsely chopped cilantro

2 tablespoons lemon juice and chopped zest

3 tablespoons finely chopped red onion

FOR THE GREMOLATA:

1. Place all of the ingredients in a large bowl.

2. Mix vigorously and allow to sit, refrigerated, for several hours. This can be done a day ahead.

4 Idaho russet potatoes

4 tablespoons fresh unsalted butter

1 bunch dandelion greens, washed clean

Kosher salt and freshly ground black pepper

FOR THE DANDELION MASHED POTATOES:

1. Preheat oven to 400°F.

2. Peel and cut the potatoes into large chunks and place in a large pot filled with cold water. Bring to a boil and then boil the potatoes for 5 minutes. Remove potatoes from the water and rinse thoroughly.

3. Place the potatoes on a parchment-lined baking sheet and roast in the oven for about 25 minutes, or until tender to the touch but not beginning to brown too much.

4. While still hot, mash the potatoes and add the butter, the dandelion greens, and salt and pepper to taste.

FOR THE LAMB LEG STEAK:

1. Marinate the steaks with good olive oil and garlic for two hours.

2. Preheat grill on high (use hard charcoal, if possible).

3. Liberally rub kosher salt, fresh ground pepper, and dried lavender all over the steaks (at least 1 tablespoon of each spread on each steak).

4. Throw steaks on the preheated grill until cooked to a perfect medium-rare (2 minutes per side of each steak). This cut of meat is tough if cooked too far. Allow the lavender to burn and make the steaks fragrant.

5. Let the steaks rest off of the grill for at least 5 minutes. Serve the steaks over a pile of dandelion mashed potatoes and top with the gremolata.

4 12-ounce lamb leg steaks

Good extra-virgin olive oil

2 cloves garlic, peeled then smashed with the side of a knife

Kosher salt and freshly ground black pepper

4 tablespoons organic dried lavender

ricotta gnocchi w. butternut squash, fried sage & sbrinz

Everyone pronounces "gnocchi" differently, and I've eaten them a few different ways as well. My favorite, though, is when they are lightly toasted in butter and served up with a simple butternut squash. Instead of potatoes, we use ricotta cheese from Calabro, which is right down the road from us in East Haven, Connecticut. Calabro whips the ricotta, giving it a lightness that comes through in the gnocchi. Don't skip the flour-sifting step in this one. We've tried it both ways—with and without the sifting—and the difference is night and day.

FEEDS: 6–8

1 butternut squash

Extra-virgin olive oil

Kosher salt and freshly ground black pepper

4 whole eggs

3 egg yolks

1½ pounds fresh ricotta

2½ cups sifted flour

2 cups flour to roll out the pasta

½ cup unsalted butter

Several leaves of fresh sage (about 12 or so)

¼-pound hunk of Sbrinz

You can substitute Parmigiano if you must, but try to find Sbrinz—it's worth it.

1. Preheat oven to 400°F.

2. Cut the squash's bottom to flatten it out so that it stands upright without falling over. With the squash upright, carefully run your knife down its sides from top to bottom, cutting away the rough, leathery skin. Cut the squash in half lengthwise and discard the seeds.

3. Cut the squash into a ½-inch dice. You'll have a good amount of pieces from just one squash. Toss the diced squash into a bowl with a good drizzle of olive oil and season with salt and pepper to taste.

4. Spread the squash out onto a parchment-lined baking sheet and place in the preheated oven for about 10–12 minutes. With a spatula, turn the squash and continue to cook for another 12–15 minutes or so, or until the squash begins to get browned and crisp. This can be done a few hours ahead, just before you incorporate it into your dish. You don't want them too mushy, just browned and caramelized.

5. In a bowl, mix the eggs and egg yolks. Once combined, add the ricotta and mix. Add the sifted flour, using a wooden spoon, and combine—you want the dough to be a gooey consistency and not overworked. Gather up the dough into a ball with floured hands and roll out into a rope or snake shape about the diameter of a quarter. The dough should be sticky; do not over use the bench flour or overwork this dough. Using a small knife, cut the rope into 1-inch "pillows."

6. Drop the pillows into a pot of boiling salted water. Remove the gnocchi 10 seconds after they begin to float to the top of the pot. Drain them, toss them with a little olive oil, and reserve in a bowl or on a sheet pan.

7. In a sauté pan over medium heat, melt the butter slowly. Wait for it to get foamy and then slowly turn to a deep golden brown color. Watch the

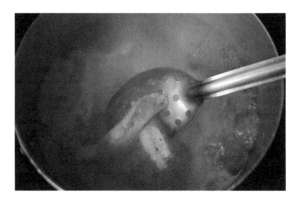

butter carefully, as you're not looking to burn it but rather just toast it. Once it's nicely toasted, add the fresh sage leaves and allow them to cook gently until nicely crisp and slightly darker. Toss in the cooked gnocchi and turn the heat up slightly. The gnocchi should begin to brown just a bit and form a nice

crust. Lastly, throw in a handful of the roasted butternut squash and toss to combine.

8. Plate up and, using a vegetable peeler, grate some large ribbons of Sbrinz on top to gently melt as you bring the gnocchi to the table.

blackened catfish w. avocado jicama salad
& chipotle chèvre quesadillas

This is probably the most recent dish we've added to the menu at Caseus that is featured in this book. It was an attempt to find a fish dish that would be affordable enough to have on the everyday menu and still be somewhat sustainable. Catfish, as it turns out, has been farmed for so long that some smaller outfits are finding ways to farm them in an ecologically sound way. As catfish are bottom-feeders and live off of the algae in the ponds, planting certain algae-producing plants can create a small, sustainable system where the fish feed the plants with their waste, the plants feed the fish, and we pan-fry the fish with blackening spice and serve as deconstructed tacos. The entire process is delicious.

FEEDS: 4

4 tablespoons hot paprika

2 tablespoons dried oregano

2 tablespoons dried thyme

2 tablespoons freshly ground black pepper

2 tablespoons cumin

2 tablespoons cayenne pepper

2 tablespoons chipotle

2 tablespoons kosher salt

FOR THE BLACKENING SPICE:

1. Mix all the ingredients together in a small bowl.

2. Allow the spices to sit together for at least a few days, if possible, before using. This may seem weird or unnecessary, but it really makes a difference if the spices have had a chance to meld.

FOR ALL THE REST:

1. Peel the jicama bulb and cut into a julienne. Cut the cabbage as thinly as possible and toss with the jicama, serranos, half of the cilantro, and the juice of 2 of the 4 limes. Season with salt and pepper and a sprinkle of blackening spice. Let sit in the fridge for about an hour.

I also love to garnish the dish with corn shoots. They are not easy to find but are a great accompaniment to the dish if you can get them. Their fresh green corn taste works wonderfully with the spiciness of the dish.

2. In a bowl, combine the fresh chèvre, about ½ pound of the queso fresco, and about half of the chipotles in adobo. With a wooden spoon, mix the two cheeses and the saucy, smoky peppers together. Smear this mixture onto the corn tortillas and grill or pan-fry them until crisp on the out-side and cheesy and melted inside. We fold them in half so everyone gets two.

3. Heat the canola oil in a large sauté pan over high heat. Dredge the fish in the blackening spice, really coating it well, and then carefully place in the hot pan. Cook the fish approximately 2 minutes on the first side and another 2 minutes on the second, or until it feels flaky. There should be a nice, dark crust forming on the fish.

4. To plate it all up, put out 4 plates and divvy up the jicama and cabbage slaw. Top each pile of slaw with half of an avocado, sliced thinly. Then add a nicely blackened fillet of catfish and two of the chipotle chèvre quesadillas. Garnish each dish with half a lime and a good sprinkle of queso fresco and cilantro.

FOR ALL THE REST:

1 bulb jicama

½ head cabbage (red or white will do)

1 fresh serrano pepper, diced

Bunch of fresh cilantro, chopped

4 limes

Kosher salt and freshly ground black pepper

¼ cup blackening spice

8 ounces fresh chèvre

¾ pound queso fresco

1 6-ounce can chipotles in adobo

8 corn tortillas

2 tablespoons canola oil

4 catfish fillets

2 ripe avocados

Extra-virgin olive oil

caseus wellington

Beef Wellington—gotta do it. Classic decadence. But tenderloin? Blech! I loathe tenderloin. Even for steak tartare, I'm just not into the cut; plus, it's just too mushy and has no real steak flavor going on. I grew up a vegetarian, so meat for me need be meaty! Besides, tenderloins are expensive, and getting the cooking time right when wrapped in pastry dough can be tricky at times. So it came to me: the everyman Wellington. At Caseus, we use our grass-fed ground beef to stuff into these wonderful pastry pockets. The foie gras melts atop them and trickles through, flavoring the ground beef for a truly sublime result.

FEEDS: 4

10 medium-size crimini mushrooms

4 slices fresh foie gras

In a pinch, you can use foie gras mousse or torchon.

2 ½-pound ground beef burgers

Kosher salt and freshly ground black pepper

1 ball of pâte brisée dough (page 18)

1 egg, beaten

Maldon salt and coarsely ground black pepper

3 pounds spinach

2 cloves garlic, smashed

About ¼ cup fresh unsalted butter

1. Preheat oven to 425°F.

2. Chop the mushrooms as finely as you can and throw them into a large heavy-bottomed sauté pan over medium heat. Cook, stirring occasionally, about half an hour. They should cook to a paste. Remove the mushrooms and wipe the pan clean.

3. Turn the heat to high and add the foie gras slices to the pan. They should melt slightly but not too much. Give them a touch of color on each side, then remove from the pan and rest atop the cooked mushrooms. You might want to open a window because the foie is going to make some serious smoke!

4. Shape the large beef burgers into high, tight trunkels or cylinders so that they are flat on two sides but higher than your typical burger. Season them heavily with kosher salt and freshly ground black pepper.

5. Using the rendered foie gras pan while still hot, sear the burgers to get a thick crust while keeping the center a cool rare. Do this quickly on both sides and then set aside out of the pan and away from the heat. Reserve the pan with the foie gras and beefy goodness now in it.

6. Working quickly, roll out the pâte brisée dough to an even thickness, about ⅛ inch or so. You won't use all of the dough, but get it all rolled out nicely and keep it cold.

7. Divide the dough into 4 large rounds, about 10 inches in diameter. Equally distribute the mushrooms onto the dough pieces, then add the foie gras and top with the seared-off burger. Pull up the dough around the burger to encase it completely, and flip it over so that the seam sits on the bottom.

8. Place the 4 Wellingtons on a parchment-lined baking sheet. Using the beaten egg and a pastry brush, or just your fingers, wash each Wellington completely. Finish with Maldon salt and coarsely ground black pepper.

9. Bake the Wellingtons in the oven for 12–18 minutes. The result should be a golden brown crust that, when opened, will yield a medium burger gushing foie gras juices.

10. Meanwhile, while the Wellingtons are cooking in the oven, sauté the spinach and garlic in the pan with the foie gras and beef juices, adding the butter as needed for more moisture and season to taste with Kosher salt and freshly ground black pepper. Let it get wilted and soft, and serve the Wellingtons over the spinach. Wellington with spinach is just a plain old winner.

larry&roz

TITLE: LD, aka The Great and Powerful Oz, and Roz

BIRTHPLACE: Yes, and for Roz . . . Connecticut

HOBBIES: Larry: National waterskiing/skeet shooting. Roz: Cooking, gardening, and reading.

FAVORITE DISH TO MAKE AT HOME: Osso bucco and risotto.

WHAT DO YOU LOVE ABOUT CASEUS? Easier to ask what don't I love . . . it's an oasis, I tell ya! The ambiance and always friendly staff.

FAVORITE CASEUS MEAL? Larry: Grits, pulled pork, guanciale and an egg. But in a pinch, lamb sliders and frites. Roz: I love the blackened catfish, the scallops over tomatoes, the soups, and, of course, the Chocolate Pot de Crème.

craig&vikki

TITLE: Faithful customers turned very good friends

BIRTHPLACE: Vikki: London, England. Craig: "Somewhere in the south."

HOBBIES: Eating, listening to music, films, shopping, viola, and roller coasters.

FAVORITE DISH TO MAKE AT HOME: Grits and shrimp jambalaya for Craig and cheese lasagna for Vikki.

WHAT DO YOU LOVE ABOUT CASEUS? Craig: Great food, wine, and company! Vikki: Nothing!

FAVORITE CASEUS MEAL? Craig: I love the grilled lamb loin with the local broccoli. Vikki: Well, I really love the pasta carbonara that you do with the house-made guanciale, but I also love the spaghetti with ramps you do once a year.

chris&liz

TITLE: Government Attorney and New Havenite, Locavore, Attorney

BIRTHPLACE: Chris: New Haven, Connecticut. Liz: Milford, Connecticut.

HOBBIES: Liz: Running, biking, swing dancing. Chris: Searching for my next meal, eating, tomfoolery, shenanigans, and hell raising in general.

FAVORITE DISH TO MAKE AT HOME: Liz: Fudge brownies and vanilla ice cream and experimenting with fresh produce from the farmers' market.

WHAT DO YOU LOVE ABOUT CASEUS? We love the proximity to our home, the noise from Trumbull Street, and the spacious dining area. We love the people and the patrons—there are lots of great, interesting people who make New Haven a fun and caring community. Jason is a rascal, too.

FAVORITE CASEUS MEAL? Chris: Grilled cheese avec jambon, pot de crème, and the Moroccan spiced lamb with quinoa salad. Liz: Pork mole tacos, lobster gazpacho, and the scallops and heirloom tomatoes.

jen&joel

TITLE: Jen: Art Director, Information Graphics, *Scientific American* magazine. Joel: Director of Development & Community Engagement (and sometimes a teacher), Common Ground.

BIRTHPLACE: Jen: Garden Grove, California. Joel: Philadelphia, Pennsylvania (repping Readfield, Maine).

HOBBIES: Eating at Caseus, cooking (somewhere less than 1 percent as well as the folks at Caseus), gardening (and then forgetting to weed), working late, sleeping on the train to NYC.

FAVORITE DISH TO MAKE AT HOME: Jen: Bacon (if Joel would let me . . . being married to a vegetarian is hard). Joel: Tacos, paella, and anything from the garden.

WHAT DO YOU LOVE ABOUT CASEUS? Joel: Everything! Before Caseus opened, I pressed my nose up against the window for about a month. (Seriously. I left marks.) Jen: Best. Bacon. Ever.

FAVORITE CASEUS MEAL? New Years 2010. It was approximately ten meals in one. Lesson learned: Order a cheeseboard on top of an eighty-course prix fixe menu, and suffer the consequences.

Chocolate Pot de Crème, 120

Goat Cheese Cheesecake, 122

Sheep's Milk Yogurt Panna Cotta, 124

Caseus Zeppoles, 126

Apple Tarts w. Cabot Clothbound Cheddar, 128

Chocolate Bacon Peanut Butter & Banana Bread Pudding, 130

Cabot Clothbound Cheddar w. Honey & Black Pepper, 132

Bucheron w. Grilled Peaches & Honey, 133

SWEETS

AT CASEUS, ALL OF OUR DESSERTS ARE HOUSE-MADE, which is why we'll usually have no more than three on the menu at any given time. Desserts should be robust, full, and most usually chocolate. Our standard is the Chocolate Pot d'Crème. It's been on the menu since we opened—it has never changed and never will. The rest of our desserts are made out of necessity. Extra brioche ends from grilled cheese sandwiches become the best bread pudding you've ever made, or for that matter ever had. If we have extra eggs one week, we make a custard. If we need to move some apples and ricotta, we make the fritter/donuts a la apple ricotta zeppoles. Usually by the time our patrons are done with their meal, they're pretty satiated, but just in case, we want our desserts to really shine. One very sweet-tooth-adorned customer orders a pot d'crème for dinner and then another for dessert. I don't recommend it, but I wouldn't argue if someone fed me two of anything that luscious and rich.

chocolate pot de crème

The one constant on the Caseus dessert menu is the chocolate pot. It is hugely popular—I have no doubt that a riot would break out if we decided not to make this ridiculously rich dessert.

FEEDS: 4

8 egg yolks

½ cup sugar

2½ cups heavy cream

½ cup milk

8 ounces bittersweet chocolate, chopped (this recipe would not work well with chocolate chips)

We use Callebaut semisweet. Use the best you can get your hands on!

Fresh whipped cream; we like this so make a ton!

1. Preheat oven to 325°F.

2. In a mixer with a paddle attachment, combine yolks and sugar and beat until nicely mixed.

3. In a large metal bowl set atop a medium-sized sauce pot with simmering water (essentially a double boiler), combine the cream, milk, and chocolate. Heat the pot so the water is simmering hot and melts the chocolate in the bowl with the cream and milk.

4. When the chocolate cream and milk mixture is nicely melted, gently fold a small amount of it into the yolk and sugar mix, tempering it slowly. Once a little of the chocolate mix is into the yolk, add the rest and whisk it to combine.

5. Pour the mixture into 10 small 4 ounce ramekins, and place them in a deep pan lined with a tea towel. Fill the pan with hot water about half way up the side of the ramekins. Bake in the oven for 20 minutes, gently turning the pan once after another 20 minutes.

The chocolate pots will jiggle slightly when moved but not ripple. This is good, as they will continue to cook after you take them out. Undercooked pots are better than dry, overcooked ones, so be brave and take the pots out earlier if they seem to be setting up quicker. Different ovens react differently.

6. Remove the chocolate pots from the oven and allow to rest overnight in the fridge, or for at least 2 hours. Serve with fresh whipped cream. We flavor our whipped cream with instant coffee to make a not-too-sweet but really robust topping for the pots.

chocolate pot de crème

goat cheese cheesecake

This is a traditional New York–style cheesecake with chèvre added. The key to the lightness of this cake, which I learned from my former bosses at Chestnut Fine Foods, is to allow it to rest in the oven overnight after baking. When you turn the oven off, the heat doesn't dissipate immediately. If you can be patient and leave the door shut, the cake continues to bake very slowly and produces an amazing light texture that cannot be beat!

FEEDS: APPROXIMATELY 12 (1 CAKE)

FOR THE CRUST:

3 cups graham cracker crumbs, hand-crushed chunky

¾ cup (1⅓ sticks) unsalted butter, melted

1. Use your hands to crush the graham crackers so they are chunky and incorporated with the melted butter.

2. Coat 9-inch springform pan with butter. Press the mixture into the bottom of the pan and about 1 inch up the sides.

3. Wrap the pan in foil halfway up the sides so that it is watertight along its bottom edge.

FOR THE FILLING:

1½ pounds cream cheese, room temperature

1 pound fresh goat chèvre, room temperature

The earlier you get these two cheeses out on your counter to warm, the better.

If you can get it, Beltane Farm's fresh chèvre is the bomb!

1 pint sour cream

2 cups sugar

Juice of ½ large lemon

1½ teaspoons vanilla extract

¼ teaspoon kosher salt

6 eggs

1. Preheat oven to 350°F.

2. In a mixer with a paddle attachment, blend all the ingredients, minus the eggs, until smooth. Then add one egg at a time, waiting until each egg incorporates fully into the mix before adding the next.

3. Blend again until smooth, stopping the mixer every so often to scrape the sides and bottom of the bowl so that there are absolutely no lumps.

TO MAKE THE CHEESECAKE:

1. Gently pour the mixture into the prepared springform pan. Place the pan in a larger pan and fill with enough water to come 1 inch up the sides of the springform pan.

2. Bake in the oven for 1¼ hours, then turn the oven off. Do not open the oven door. Allow the cake to sit in the oven overnight, or at least 8 hours.

3. Remove the cake from the springform pan. Refrigerate the cake overnight or for at least 6 hours. This cake improves if allowed to sit around, and is at its best the second or third day after baking. Serve with berries, peaches, or just about anything. It's sweet and tangy and delicious.

ann&joe

TITLE: Nana and Poppy

BIRTHPLACE: New Haven, Connecticut

HOBBIES: Sketching, knitting, reading, watching movies, cars, and photography.

FAVORITE DISH TO MAKE AT HOME: Puttanesca sauce for pasta, and pork chops with tomato sauce (that was how Poppy's mother used to make them). Upside-down cakes for family occasions with lots of variations of nuts and fruit, depending on the season.

WHAT DO YOU LOVE ABOUT CASEUS? Poppy: My grandson owns it! Nana: Ooooh . . . everything!

FAVORITE CASEUS MEAL? Nana: Mussels and onion soup, with the beet salad a close second. Poppy: The Poppy Special, which changes all the time, but is some form of grilled steak with cheese and a very spicy sauce. It's made just for me—it's not on the menu.

lucy

TITLE: Grama or Bapchi Sobo

BIRTHPLACE: Milford, Connecticut

HOBBIES: Watching the birds and old TV shows.

FAVORITE DISH TO MAKE AT HOME: Galumpkis (stuffed cabbage).

WHAT DO YOU LOVE ABOUT CASEUS? It's owned by my grandson! It's a very friendly place. The food is excellent and it's good service.

FAVORITE CASEUS MEAL? Steak Frites.

sheep's milk yogurt panna cotta

Whenever we make panna cotta at Caseus, it sells like mad and our customers rave about it. Lenny, one of our cooks, played around with this recipe, slowly reducing the amount of gelatin until the consistency resembled more of a custard than the firmer, stiffer dessert people may be used to. The sheep's milk yogurt gives the dish a great tang and a truly rich robustness. We use Old Chatham sheep's milk yogurt from New York, which is available in some supermarkets, but any rich yogurt will do.

FEEDS: 1 PER PERSON

1 quart heavy cream

2½ tablespoons gelatin

2½ cups sheep's milk yogurt

2 teaspoons real vanilla extract

1 cup sugar

Pinch of kosher salt

1. Pour about 2 tablespoons of the heavy cream into a small saucepan with the gelatin. Bloom the gelatin over medium heat and allow it to come to a simmer, but not a hard boil. Watch it. The cream and gelatin can get overdone quickly, and then it is ruined. Gently simmer for a few minutes to dissolve the gelatin completely. Let it sit off the stove for a few minutes to cool slightly.

2. Pour the remaining ingredients into a large bowl and whisk to combine, fully incorporating the sugar into the cream and yogurt.

3. Slowly add the now-bloomed gelatin to the large bowl and whisk to combine completely.

4. Pour the mixture into a dozen or so 5- or 6-ounce cups. Place in the refrigerator for a minimum of 6 hours.

   We use small foil cups, which can be used over and over again but are convenient and easy to un-mold. Some recipes call for these to be sprayed with cooking spray. We usually don't do this, but you can if you feel they will not un-mold nicely.

5. Gently un-mold the cups onto individual plates and top with your favorite seasonal fruit or fruit preserves.

caseus zeppoles

Zeppole is a traditional Italian pastry that is usually made during the Feast of St. Joseph. At Caseus, we make them year-round, changing the flavors with the season. Our most popular are simple lemon zeppoles—light and crisp on the outside, with a warm, slightly dense, and chewy dough center. The secret to this dish is to use great ricotta and never to use a mixer or even a spoon or spatula. Your hands make for the least amount of work on the supersensitive dough.

FEEDS: ENOUGH FOR 1 MEDIUM-SIZED GROUP OR 1 SERIOUS DONUT LOVER!

2 quarts peanut oil

⅛ cup sugar

2⅛ cups flour

⅛ teaspoon baking powder

Pinch of salt

Zest of 1 lemon

2 cups fresh ricotta

1 teaspoon vanilla

4 eggs

2 cups powdered sugar

1. In a deep heavy-bottomed pot, heat the peanut oil to about 375°F.

2. Combine the dry ingredients (minus the powdered sugar) and lemon zest in a bowl. Make a hole in the dry mixture and add the ricotta, vanilla, and eggs inside of the well you've created. Combine with your hands, mixing gently until just slightly sticking together.

3. Ball loosely by pinching a golf-ball-size glob into your fingertips.

4. Quickly, but very carefully, drop the globs into the hot oil. Do not add more than five globs to the pot at a time. Fry until nicely golden to dark brown and puffed on the outside. They should take about 5–6 minutes per batch.

5. While hot, toss the zeppoles in a bowl of powdered sugar. Serve immediately. The dish is best when eaten within minutes of coming out of the fryer.

apple tarts w. cabot clothbound cheddar

I first heard of this combination several years ago when I did a cheese and poetry class. Eugene Fields wrote a poem called "Apple Pie and Cheese," and the combination is inherently New England. The combination of the two will take the most mundane apple pie to new levels, particularly when a great cheddar is melted on top. Here we do a classic French-style apple tart. Simple in its preparation and execution, the key is to use sharp farmhouse-style cheddar. My favorite is Cabot Clothbound Cheddar, a collaboration between Cabot and the brothers Andy and Mateo at Jasper Hill Farm. The cheese is big, sweet, and spiced, and is so wonderful that I suggest getting extra for snacking on while making this recipe.

FEEDS: 4

1 ball of pâte brisée dough (page 18)

4 large good apples

Local is best. For this recipe, I like the tartness of a Granny Smith.

4 tablespoons unsalted butter, melted

1 teaspoon cinnamon

Pinch of dried ginger

1 tablespoon raw sugar

This is also known as turbinado sugar. It still has the molasses in it and has a larger granular form.

About 1 pound Cabot Clothbound Cheddar

If you can't find this amazing gem, go for another great cheddar, such as Grafton Stone House, Neal's Yard Dairy Keen's, or Montgomery's cheddars.

1. Preheat oven to 400°F.

2. Roll out the pâte brisée dough to around ¼ inch in thickness. Make 4 tart shells with the dough using 4 6-inch tart rings, raising the edges up about 1 inch from the bottom of the tart shell.

3. Slice the apples thinly and fan the apple slices out in each tart shell. Brush each tart with melted butter and then sprinkle with the cinnamon, ginger, and raw sugar. Bake in the oven until the crust is nicely browned, about 10–15 minutes.

4. Top each tart with the cheddar cheese, crumbled into hazelnut-size pieces and divided evenly. Place back in the oven for a few minutes, until the cheese is nicely melted but not too runny.

5. Remove the tarts from the oven and let rest for about 10 minutes. Serve with champagne or a sparkling hard cider.

chocolate bacon peanut butter & banana bread pudding

This is a spin on Elvis's classic peanut butter, bacon, and banana sandwich, which you should make an effort to experience, if you haven't already. The nutty, sticky peanut butter mixed with the salty, crisp bacon and sweet banana just plain works. Encased in velvety rich and crisp bits of custardy bread and dark chocolate, this dessert rocks. When chocolate is used as the ingredient to tame things down, you know you're on the right track. One of our chefs, Nate, came up with the idea to create sandwiches and then cut them up and soak them in custard. The result is a marbled bread pudding with pockets of each ingredient suspended throughout for that perfect bite.

FEEDS: 6

1 loaf brioche

2 cups unsalted peanut butter

1 or 2 of your favorite dark chocolate bars

2 bananas

1 pound bacon, cooked until nicely crisp (reserve the fat)

1 quart heavy cream

4 eggs

1 tablespoon real vanilla extract

1 cup brown sugar

Pinch of kosher salt

1. Preheat oven to 375°F.

2. Slice the brioche loaf into several 1-inch slices. Lay the slices out on a table and begin to make sandwiches.

3. Spread each sandwich with some peanut butter, a few pieces of the chocolate bar, some banana slices, and a few strips of bacon. Once the sandwiches are complete, cut each one into quarters. Grease a deep 9 x 13-inch pan with the rendered bacon fat and put the cut-up sandwiches in the pan.

4. In a large bowl, combine the cream, eggs, vanilla, brown sugar, and salt, and whisk until nicely combined. This is your custard.

5. Pour most, but not all, of the custard over the sandwich pieces in the pan. Using your hand in a clawlike motion, gently work the custard into the bread, slowly adding all of the custard. Let sit for about an hour. If the sandwiches have soaked up all of the custard, you'll need to add more. Combine 1 egg and 1 cup of cream and add to the pan. Let soak some more. If it still soaks it all up, repeat until you have very wet sandwiches. Sometimes the bread needs none, but sometimes it needs 2 or 3 more additions of custard.

6. Spray the top of the bread pudding with cooking spray and then cover tightly with foil. Bake in the oven for 30–45 minutes. Check it once. It should be puffing slightly and getting slightly firmer but not dry.

7. Remove the pan from the oven and take off the foil. Place the pudding back in the oven to allow to finish cooking for another 15–20 minutes, or until nicely browned on top.

8. Allow to rest for about 2 hours before cutting and serving. Serve hot by cutting pieces and reheating them in a 400°F oven for a few minutes, and then top with freshly whipped cream.

cabot clothbound cheddar w. honey & black pepper

Less a recipe and more a classic idea, the combination of the briny, salty Cheddar with the sweet honey and spiced black pepper is just a plain home run.

FEEDS: 4

½ pound Cabot Clothbound Cheddar

For this recipe, I like to use an aged cheese, at least 1 1/2 years old.

About ¼ cup good honey

We use a local honey, Swords into Plowshares, which is made directly around the corner from us less than a quarter mile away.

Tellicherry black pepper

Tellicherry is our standard for good, fresh black pepper. Get it in whole peppercorn form and use a classic pepper grinder that has the ability to allow you a finer or coarser grind. This tool is a must-have in any kitchen, and good black pepper is an essential spice for every dish. The pepper is not even really spicy but more spiced and nutty in this dish.

1. Crumble the cheese into large chunks, about the size of a quarter or half dollar.

2. Bring the cheese to the table with the jar of honey and the freshly loaded pepper grinder. Drizzle the honey all over the cheese, followed by a few good grinds of pepper, and you've just made the simplest, most wonderfully delicious dessert around.

If you have them and you're looking to use them up, fresh black truffles are a wonderful addition to the dish. Lambrusco is the perfect wine to enjoy with this dessert.

bucheron w. grilled peaches & honey

When you can get them ripe, grilling peaches is about the best thing to do to them. The sugars caramelize and char on the grill, making a crunchy, sweet, fruity crust. To cut the sweetness of the grilled fruit, classic goat's milk chèvre in the shape of a log, known as Bucheron—which means "log" or "logger"—is creamy, acidic, and classic Loire Valley all the way. Add a touch of local honey to marry the cheese and fruit, and you've got summer's most sought-after dessert. The best way to make this dish is to use coals left over from cooking your main meal. I like to put the peaches on the grill as it's dying down and just leave them on until I'm ready for dessert. The slow grilling produces a great crust and imparts a wonderful smokiness.

FEEDS: 4

1. Let the cheese sit on the counter to get up to room temperature. This dessert just does not work with cold cheese, straight from the fridge.

2. Halve the peaches and remove the pits. Drizzle them with a little olive oil and then, using your hands, rub it in. This is to help prevent them from sticking to the grill.

3. Give the peaches a nice, good grill. Don't move them around much. You should really only move them once, and that is to remove them from the grill. This way they have time to caramelize.

4. Once off the grill, throw a few nice hunks of the gooey room-temperature Bucheron onto the peach halves and drizzle with honey. I like a ton of fresh cracked pepper on them. The dish pairs well with a nice light beer, like Ayinger from Germany.

½ pound ripe Bucheron

2 large ripe peaches

Extra-virgin olive oil

¼ cup good raw local honey

I don't like to use dark honey for this but rather the lightest honey I can find that is local, fresh, and raw.

Freshly ground black pepper (optional)

BUILDING BLOCKS

CASEUS

GOOD INGREDIENTS ARE THE FOUNDATIONS OF ALL GREAT CUISINE. The starting components of any dish must be as good as the finished dish itself. Most of these recipes have fairly basic preparation. Others take time to simmer on the stove while you plan your menu, return some e-mails, and oil your butcher block. Substituting store-bought stock for homemade is perfectly suitable if, that is, you want your food to be devoid of heart, love, and integrity. Much like raising children, cooking is about taking the time to truly nurture your food, care for it. If you decide not to do this, you will get back what you give. I don't need to harp on this any more than I have. Make it right, and if you can't make it right, then come to Caseus and eat it right.

cured lemons

You must make this recipe. If you do not make this simple recipe, you are lazy and worthless—but I'll still love you. It's just so simple and yields such great flavor that I really am adamant about you making this! We use these amazing lemons year-round in a ton of our recipes, from sweets to savories. They're truly a building block component essential in a plethora of dishes.

3 large shallots

5 cloves fresh garlic

3 tablespoons sugar

3 tablespoons kosher salt

4 good, clean lemons

1. Peel and dice the shallots and garlic as fine as possible but not into a paste. Mix the sugar and salt together.

2. Using a mandolin, slicer, or knife, cut the ends off of each lemon and discard.

3. Slice the lemons thinly and layer them in a single layer in a medium-size Mason or Ball jar with a lid. Sprinkle just a bit of the diced shallot and garlic and the salt and sugar mixture onto the layer of lemons. Repeat this until all of the lemons are stacked in the jar.

4. Press the lemons down so that they are nicely compact. Close the jar and refrigerate for about 3 weeks. Every so often, turn the jar upside down for a few seconds so that the juices released from the lemons are evenly distributed. After a few weeks, you can use the cured lemons in a ton of different recipes.

chicken stock

This is a brown chicken stock, not a white chicken stock. All of the recipes in this book that call for chicken stock call for brown chicken stock. White or clear chicken stock has its place, but not at Caseus. Browning the bones and carcasses before making the stock brings out the rustic, sweet robustness of the chicken. White stock, commonly used for fancy sauces and such, has the hint of poultry dancing gingerly around the back of the flavor profile. My stock is always brown.

---

1. Preheat oven to 400°F.

2. Roast the chicken bones, carcasses, etc., in a roasting pan in the oven for about 1½ hours, turning them once or twice to evenly brown them on all sides.

3. Put the roasted bones and all of the other ingredients in a deep stock pot, and top with enough water to cover the bones and veggies. Let simmer over medium to low, but not come to a full boil, for at least 4 hours.

4. Strain, and allow the stock to cool overnight in the fridge so that you can skim off the fat. You can use this fat to cook up everything from livers to eggs! Now you have nice chicken stock. This version is lighter, so for a richer stock, after you've strained out the vegetables, you can reduce the stock further. Don't add salt until it is completely finished, if ever. Taste it first to see if it needs any.

The dish that the stock is going to be used in will likely have salt in it, so there really is no reason to salt stock at all.

3 pounds chicken bones, carcasses, necks, and backs

These can be left over from your roast chicken, your chicken wings from the game, etc.

1 onion, skin on and cut in half

2 celery stalks, leaves on

1 carrot, unpeeled and cut in half

2 cloves garlic, skin on and cut in half

1 tablespoon peppercorns

1 cup heirloom bomb (page 145) or 1 tablespoon good tomato paste

¼ bulb fresh fennel (optional)

2 cups good dry white wine

Don't use something you wouldn't drink, but if you have wine kicking around you've not used up, that would be the perfect choice. I like a Muscadet for this, if available.

Enough water to cover the bones (you'll need to gauge this to your pot size)

A FEW QUICK WORDS ON STOCKS:

Make your own.

Make it in large batches.

Pack it in small batches.

Freeze it for convenient use.

Never use store-bought.

Never, ever, under any circumstances, use powder or concentrated stocks.

beef stock

Approximately 3 pounds beef trimmings

We use the trimmings off of our skirt steaks and any other steak trimmings we have. When you trim any beef, save the scraps and freeze them so that you have a nice pile to make your stock with. If you don't have beef trimmings, use oxtails as they are cheap and easy to find at our local butcher.

1 onion, skin on and cut in half

2 celery stalks, leaves on and cut in half

1 carrot, unpeeled and cut in half

2 cloves garlic, skin on and cut in half

1 tablespoon peppercorns

1 cup heirloom bomb (page 145) or 1 tablespoon good tomato paste

¼ bulb fresh fennel (optional)

2 cups good dry red wine

Don't use something you wouldn't drink, but if you have wine kicking around you've not used up, that would be the perfect choice.

Enough water to cover your scraps or oxtails(you'll need to gauge this to your pot size and how much trimmings you've got)

1. Preheat oven to 400°F.

2. Roast the trimmings in a roasting pan in the oven for about 1½ hours, turning them once or twice and moving them around to evenly brown them on all sides.

3. Put the trimmings, pan juices, and any yummy bits scraped off of the pan as well as all of the other ingredients in a deep stock pot, and top with enough water to cover the roasted beef trimmings and veggies. Let simmer over medium to low, but not come to a full boil, for at least 4 hours.

4. Strain, and let cool in the fridge until the fat rises enough to be skimmed off the top. Save this and fry just about anything, but especially potatoes in beef fat! Now you have nice beefy stock. This version is lighter. For a richer stock, after you've strained out the vegetables, you can reduce the stock further. Don't add salt until it is completely finished, if ever. Taste it first to see if it needs any.

The dish that the stock is going to be used in will likely have salt in it, so there really is no reason to salt stock at all.

What can I say about homemade stock? To my mind, it is one of the main reasons (along with the amount of butter used) why restaurant food tastes so much richer than most home-cooked foods. Making a batch of this stuff and reducing it down to pure gold glace is a huge statement in your culinary lifestyle. Your food will be more robust, more flavorful and true, than ever before.

veal stock

1. Preheat oven to 400°F.

2. Roast the veal bones in the oven in a roasting pan for about 1½ hours, turning them once or twice to evenly brown them on all sides.

3. Put the roasted bones and all of the other ingredients in a deep stock pot, and top with enough water to cover the bones and veggies. Let simmer over medium to low, but not come to a full boil, for at least 4 hours.

4. Strain, and let cool in your fridge until you can skim off the fat. Veal fat is awesome to fry up just about anything, especially Jerusalem artichokes. Now you have nice veal stock. This version is lighter. For a richer stock, after you've strained out the vegetables, you can reduce the stock further. Don't add salt until it is completely finished, if ever. Taste it first to see if it needs any.

The dish that the stock is going to be used in will likely have salt in it, so there really is no reason to salt stock at all.

At Caseus, we don't freeze our stocks because we go through them so quickly. Monday and Tuesday are our building block days. Since we don't have dinner service on those days, we start preparing stocks, sauces, mayonnaise, dressings, and cured lemons, as well as a slew of other building blocks to use throughout the rest of the week. By not having to prep the kitchen for dinner service, the oven, grill, and counter space is available for us to get those large, time-consuming prep items out of the way. Do this at home for yourself when planning your weekly meals. Or put down this book and pick up the phone and make a reservation at Caseus. You won't have to do any cooking or cleaning!

Approximately 3 pounds veal bones, cut into small pieces (you will most likely have to get these frozen)

1 onion, skin on and cut in half

2 celery stalks, leaves on and cut in half

1 carrot, unpeeled and cut in half

2 cloves garlic, skin on and cut in half

1 tablespoon peppercorns

1 cup heirloom bomb (page 145) or 1 tablespoon good tomato paste

¼ bulb fresh fennel (optional)

2 cups good dry red wine

Don't use something you wouldn't drink, but if you have wine kicking around you've not used up, that would be the perfect choice.

Enough water to cover the bones (you'll need to gauge this to your pot size and how many bones you have)

sangria . . . caseus cool-aid

A customer review on the website Yelp coined the name Caseus Cool-Aid for our wonderful sangria. We serve all of our wines by the glass, not just by the bottle. The idea is that you can come in and try out a few, learn about them, and have some fun while getting informed and drunk. But then, at the end of the night, we're left with thirty to forty bottles of opened wine. What do we do? We mix them into sangria!

---

2 lemons

2 limes

2 oranges

2 8-ounce glass bottles Coca-Cola Classic

½ cup simple syrup

1½ cups tawny port

Top off with a mix of 4 750-millileter bottles of decent dry red wine

1. Cut the citrus fruits in half, then in quarters, and then into little slices to make small bite-size triangles. Place the triangles in a large bowl, or, if you have a gallon pickle jar, that works great.

2. Mix all of the ingredients together and let sit in the fridge for at least 30 minutes. Taste it. It might need a bit more port if you like it sweeter. Or it might need another bottle of Coke. I like it fizzy and will often throw in a bottle of Gassosa, a lemon-lime soda from Foxon Park.

3. Serve over ice with the fruit sitting on top for easy access to munch and suck on.

Use what you have. You know you have one bottle kicking around that someone gave you that you'll never drink. Use that bottle and three other decent ones.

house mayonnaise

Growing up, my subs usually had oil and vinegar instead of mayo as a condiment because I never liked the odd slick that coated my mouth when eating regular mayonnaise. When I got older and tried freshly made mayo for the first time, all of that changed, and now I think of excuses to use our fresh mayo. Nothing beats it on fresh, hot fries.

1. In a food processor or blender, combine the eggs, dry mustard, salt, pepper, and lemon juice.

2. With the food processor or blender on high speed, slowly drizzle the canola oil into the machine until all the ingredients are emulsified. Do this as slowly as possible. Remove the mayo into a bowl and cover, letting it rest in the fridge for at least 2 hours. Store it for no more than 3 days.

2 local egg yolks

They must be as fresh as you can possibly get them for this recipe.

1 teaspoon dry mustard

Pinch of kosher salt and a few heavy grinds of fresh cracked black pepper

I like to tighten up the grinder and make the pepper a bit finer for this so I don't get large hunks of pepper in the mayo.

1 tablespoon lemon juice

1 cup canola oil

Do not substitute olive oil, as it makes the mayo a heavy slick.

sherry vinaigrette

It's a simple dressing for everything from salads to pastas.

1 lemon, zested then juiced (do this in the right order or it's much harder)

¼ cup Pedro Ximenez sherry vinegar

¾ cup extra-virgin olive oil

Dash of Maldon salt

Freshly ground black pepper

1 teaspoon Dijon mustard

1. Combine the juice of the lemon, the zest, and the Pedro Ximenez sherry vinegar together in a bowl and begin whisking.
2. Slowly add the olive oil in a very thin stream while vigorously whisking.
3. Add Dijon mustard, then salt and pepper to taste.

Both vinaigrettes can be stored for up to 2 weeks.

cured lemon vinaigrette

This is our Caseus house *vin*. We use it on everything! This batch makes one full quart of dressing; enough for at least a week's worth of salads and anything else you can think to put this on.

4 lemons, juiced

1 small shallot

1 clove garlic

1 cup cider vinegar

1 cup champagne vinegar

Pinch of kosher salt and freshly ground black pepper

1 tablespoon sugar

1 cup canola oil

1¼ cups extra-virgin olive oil

1. Combine the first eight ingredients in a blender and let 'er whip!
2. Drizzle in the canola oil followed by the olive oil very slowly to make a nice, smooth dressing.
3. Use after a week and a half, and keep in the refrigerator until about an hour before using.

Awesome on fish!

heirloom bomb

This is another one of those procedures more so than a recipe. But in the height of summer tomato season, this is a great way to preserve that bright tomato taste and use up some of your not-so-pretty tomatoes.

1. Cut the tomatoes into large chunks and spread them onto a baking sheet lined with parchment paper.

2. Season them lightly with the salt and pepper, then pop them into an oven at the lowest heat; 175°F or 200°F will do.

3. Let them cook for at least ten hours; preferably 12. We do this overnight.

4. Drain off the excess water and save it for making gazpacho or anything else you like (it's great added to vodka).

5. Combine the wrinkled chunks into a blender or food processor and blend 'till smooth.

6. Freeze in small batches that are easy to use.

As many older, bruised-up or beaten tomatoes as you have.

We use the ones with spots and cut out any undesirable pieces.

Kosher salt and freshly ground black pepper

Great for tomato soup, sauces, and just about anything that needs a bright summer tomato punch when great tomatoes aren't in season.

CRUCIAL COOKING CHEESES

Listed in no particular order, our go-to cheeses:

COMTÉ: The king in my eyes, this cheese is the best ever for cooking, melting, or eating straight up. Versatile, oniony, sweet, not too soft, not too hard—this French Jura Mountains pressed cured cheese is one of my favorites. I love Comté and eat it often in any season and use it for any occasion. It's always a crowd pleaser. It's moderate to high in price but spot-on consistent in quality.

The best, the one we use at Caseus, is the Comté St. Antoine from Marcel Petit. The legendary affineur uses an abandoned munitions fort once used to stave off invaders coming through Switzerland to house its cheeses for the twelve- to sixteen-month-long maturation into eighty pounds of perfect nutty creaminess.

GOUDA: We use a few good cooking Goudas, the Dutch standard cow's milk cheese, wheel-aged a minimum of one year. Our two favorites are Old Amsterdam and Beemster Vlaskaas. They are sweet and nutty, melt well, and give a bit of color to our dishes with their bright orange hue. The sweetness of the Goudas comes from a process called washing the curds. This is done when the cheese is separated into curds and whey, and the whey is drained from the vat. Fresh water is then added to the vat and the curds are essentially washed. The washing removes lactic acid and leaves the aged cheese with a sweetness that is great in grilled cheese, mac and cheese, and atop onion soup.

RACLETTE: This classic raw cow's milk cheese is made in France and Switzerland and is named for the way it is melted. We love the stinky unctuousness it adds when mixed in with other cheeses. This cheese gets people's nose attention!

EXTRA-SHARP VERMONT CHEDDAR: We use Grafton cheddar, made from unpasteurized Jersey cow's milk. It takes ten pounds of milk to make one pound of the cheese and, although it doesn't melt wonderfully and tends to separate a bit, its sharpness just can't be beat on a burger or mixed into mac and cheese.

FOURME D'AMBERT: This creamy raw milk blue from the Auvergne region in France has been made since ancient times. It is one of the best blue cheeses around for melting, and although it is not the most robust blue, its spiciness intensifies as it's melted. Its spongy texture is perfect to top off a burger.

FONTINA VAL D'AOSTA: This cow's milk cheese from the Aosta region of Italy is a great melting cheese. The cows graze on regional herbs and grasses, which can be tasted in the cheese. A bit of stench comes through when heated, and it produces those wonderful strings we all love to stretch into our mouths

MORBIER HAUT-JURA: This is a traditional cheese from France made from raw cow's milk with a line of ash running through to separate the morning and evening milk. This one can be a real stinker. Its texture is much like Raclette or Fontina but a bit smoother in consistency. It's wonderful for open-face melting on bread to accompany soups.

CAVE-AGED GRUYÈRE: This raw cow's milk cheese from Switzerland is washed in brine as it ages, during

which time its sweet and nutty flavor becomes more assertive. It is a must to top off onion soup and in mac and cheese. It's a wonderful go-to cheese for just about everything from melting to eating raw.

FRESH CHEESE CURDS: Made from fresh young cheeses before they are pressed into blocks or aged, curds can be used as snacks or the base for several popular dishes, such as poutine. We also like to add this to grilled cheese for that stretchy stringiness. Its flavor is not pronounced, so it often needs another cheese to accompany it.

SHEEP'S MILK FETA: We use Valbreso feta from France, made with microbial rennet. Less salty and briny than most feta, this cheese is almost sweet and very bright. It's great to add to salads and to finish dishes.

BUCHERON: This versatile goat's milk cheese log is made in France. It has two distinct textures: a half inch of cream line forms beneath the bloomy rind, while the center has a paste-like texture with a rich lemon tang. Add to mixes for mac and cheese or any melting mix to get that distinctive tang that can lighten a dish considerably.

RESOURCES

Because Caseus is so small and we just don't have the room or infrastructure to be able to have an internet business, I recommend that you check out Formaggio Kitchen. They have the best selection and ability to ship anywhere in the country.
www.formaggiokitchen.com

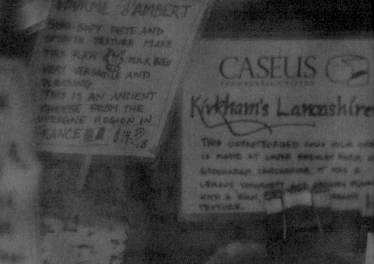

FOURME d'AMBERT

ITS SOFT PASTE AND
SMOOTH TEXTURE MAKE
THIS RAW MILK BLEU
VERY VERSATILE AND
PLEASANT.
THIS IS AN ANCIENT
CHEESE FROM THE
AUVERGNE REGION IN
FRANCE $14.⁹⁵

CASEUS

Kirkham's Lancashire

THIS UNPASTEURISED COWS MILK CHEESE
IS MADE AT LOWER BEESLEY FARM AT
GOOSNARGH, LANCASHIRE. IT HAS A
LEMONY YOGHURTY AND ACIDIC FLAVOUR
WITH A SOFT AND CRUMBLY
TEXTURE.

CASEUS CO
St Agur

CASEUS GruyEre Reserve
CASEUS
FROMAGERIE • BISTRO

THIS COW'S MILK CHEESE IS MADE
IN SWITZERL

CASEUS PASTEURIZED
FROMAGERIE • BISTRO
nken GOAT
0 de Murcia al vino)
ft goats milk cheese
in Monast
ent
22.00 lb

ACKNOWLEDGMENTS

I'VE ALWAYS WANTED TO WRITE A COOKBOOK, and what better way than to have it coupled with my bistro and cheese shop to remind everyone, myself included, how much work, passion, drive, and pure luck has gone into making Caseus what it is today. To write an acknowledgments page thanking all of those that add value to Caseus would be ridiculously long. So for everyone I miss, know that I am forever grateful for your contributions.

To our first Chef Fabrice for helping me open the kitchen; our second Chef Chris for helping the kitchen step out of a French Bistro and into a Gastropub; and our current amazing team of Joe, Nate, Lenny, Steve, Jay, Uriel, Miguel, and Victor for making Caseus the best little kitchen around. You guys all amaze me daily!

To our cheesemongers Andrew, Lydia, Meredith, and our servers and managers Tim, Chris, Krystal, Dan, Simone, Mike, Aura, Amanda, Thumpy G, Chutch, Hailey, Alley, and Sarah—you guys make this place what it is daily, and for that I thank you! You're passion for food, especially cheese, has made Caseus a great place not only to come eat, but to learn and admire true artisan products.

To my parents, Tom and Sylvia, who let me mortgage their house to raise some of the funds to open Caseus when no banks would touch me—you painted and garbage-picked oak wood to help build the bar, brought pizza to me on those long nights, and so much more. You're thanked every time you come in here and eat . . . usually for free. So that's taken care of.

To my grandparents, Grama Sobo, Nana and Poppy, who lent me more cash to be able to open up—you helped stain tables and chairs, went on runs to Home Depot for glue and screws, and gave me the love of food as a child with your wonderful cooking. You guys eat here all the time, too! So that's taken care of.

To my friends Omar, Steve, John, Cliffdog, Dan, Misza, Mario, Bird, Moles, and so many more I just don't have room to mention—for all your support over the years, letting me cook for you, and experiment on you with my food. You guys come and drink for free all the time! So you're taken care of.

To Patty and Fred Walker of Chestnut Fine Foods who taught me the most crucial parts of the food industry: to love your job, do it well, and work your ass off. You guys do not come in often enough because you're working too much . . . so get in here and have some free food and booze already! I owe you!

To my Formaggio Kitchen Family, Robert, Phil, Bob, Greg, Ishan, Kurt, Edwardo, Alice, Tom, Michael, Christine, and so many more for being friends, educators, mentors, and all around amazing people submerged in the best damn food I've yet experienced. You all live too far away to come take advantage of free food and booze, so I thank you for that, too.

To my little brother, Tom, who came home from college to help me run this crazy place and make it something truly wonderful. Your thanks will come in dollars someday—be patient, keep the faith.

To my beautiful wife, Kelly, who told me I could do anything I wanted as long as I asked her first, for kicking my ass, for not letting me quit or bitch or get down, for being there every time I needed you, and for carrying around our soon to be born (as I write this 7/14/11) little offspring, SuperHawk Sobocinski.

I love each and every one of you very much and will forever be in your debt.

Thank you all for everything!

INDEX

ABOUT THE AUTHOR

JASON SOBOCINSKI, the owner and creator of New Haven's award-winning restaurant/cheese shop Caseus Fromagerie Bistro, comes from a long line of Italian food merchants and a family of food lovers. A graduate of Providence College, he earned his masters degree in Gastronomy at Boston University and worked his way up the ranks at the prestigious Formaggio Kitchen in Cambridge. Armed with lots of cheesy knowledge, he opened Caseus in New Haven, Connecticut (www.caseusnewhaven.com). With his innovative cheese-centered gastropub, Jason has succeeded in "extending our kitchen table" to welcome a steady stream of happy customers. He lives in Hamden, Connecticut.